Cybersex
Unhooked

ALSO BY DAVID DELMONICO, PH.D., ELIZABETH GRIFFIN, M.A.,
AND JOSEPH MORIARITY, B.A., B.S.

In the Shadows of the Net: Breaking Free of
Compulsive Online Sexual Behavior
 (with Patrick Carnes, Ph.D.)

ALSO BY JOSEPH MORIARITY
Winning a Day at a Time
 (with John Lucas)
Sexual Anorexia: Overcoming Sexual Self-Hatred
 (with Patrick Carnes, Ph.D.)

Cybersex Unhooked

A Workbook for Breaking Free of Compulsive Online Sexual Behavior

David Delmonico, Ph.D.,   Elizabeth Griffin, M.A.,   Joseph Moriarity

Gentle Path
P R E S S

WICKENBURG, ARIZONA

GENTLE PATH PRESS
P.O. Box 3345
Wickenburg, AZ 85358
www.gentlepath.com
800-955-9853

Library of Congress Cataloging-in-Publication Data
Delmonico, David, Griffin, Elizabeth, and Moriarity, Joseph
    Cybersex Unhooked: A Workbook for Breaking Free of Compulsive Online Sexual Behavior/David Delmonico . . . [et al.].
p. cm.
Includes bibliographical references.
ISBN: 0-9708845-0-8
1. Sex Addiction. 2. Recovery.

Authors' note:
The stories in this book are true; however, each has been edited for clarity. Names, locations, and other identifying information have been changed to protect confidentiality.

Cover and interior design by Theresa Gedig
Set in Berling

Printed by Bang Printing, Brainerd, Minnesota

Acknowledgments

We would like to extend our heartfelt thanks to the following for their contributions to this manuscript:

Dr. Patrick Carnes, for the tremendous contributions he has made not only in the field of sexual addiction but also in the addiction field as a whole. His pioneering research and writing has been a powerful force in creating an acceptance of sex addiction as a disease rather than a perversion. We are also grateful for his invaluable advice, insight, and guidance.

Project Pathfinder, Inc., for allowing us to adapt and use a number of recovery exercises. Project Patherfinder is a nonprofit organization whose vision—"dedicated to the elimination of sexual violence and abuse"—is grounded in the belief that sexually abusive behavior can be treated and that prevention programs can reduce the incidence of abuse.

Robin Kato, executive director of the National Council on Sex Addiction and Compulsivity, for her creative contributions to the development of the RecoveryHex model.

Jerry Fjerkenstad, for creating and sharing the Hermes' Web concept and materials.

Authors' Notes

This workbook was written in part to serve as a companion to the book, *In the Shadows of the Net: Breaking Free of Compulsive Online Sexual Behavior*, which was written with Patrick Carnes, Ph.D., and is published by Hazelden (www.hazelden.org).

We suggest that you consider reading this book as well, since it offers additional information about problematic cybersex behavior and recovery that you will find valuable in your work. Topics in the book that may interest you include the stages of courtship, patterns of sexual arousal and ways they change, setting appropriate relationship boundaries, relapse prevention, the impact of cybersex on the family, and the Web frontier.

Contents

CHAPTER 1: *Sharing Our Stories*

At the time, it probably seemed like a dream come true—your discovery of sex on the Internet. You'd already been impressed by all that the Internet had to offer: information, goods, connections, and more. And there was sex, too. Sex on the Internet—whenever you want with exactly the kind of person you want.

Eventually, you began to think that perhaps, for you, sex on the Internet was too good to be true. The opportunity is too enticing, alluring, fulfilling, immediate, and powerful. So much is available. There are so many options, ones you've only dreamed of—or had yet to dream of! So much opportunity and stimulation is available that it's difficult to control. And hard to stop. Maybe, it seems, impossible to stop.

Yes, the Net does have a shadow side. For some people, the pull of cybersex can be so powerful, that, as with alcohol or other drugs, it's hard to control or stop.

You may be wondering whether you're alone in this struggle with sex and the Internet. You're not. The shadowy world of cybersex is overtaking and overwhelming far too many people, undermining careers and upending relationships. And the problem is growing. For some, cybersex becomes compulsive, even addictive. No one could have forecast that cybersex would have such an impact.

Countless people, men and women alike, find themselves in what seems to be a futile struggle with online sexual behavior. Mostly they struggle alone and in silence, too embarrassed or guilt-ridden to seek help, not knowing where they can find help, believing that no one else would really understand anyway. Each day brings a roller coaster of emotions. Perhaps you are in a similar predicament. Have you ever done any of the following?

- kept sexual activity on the Internet a secret from family members
- carried out sexual activities on the Net at work
- frequently found yourself erasing your computer-history files in an effort to conceal your activity on the Net

- felt ashamed at the thought that someone you love might discover your Internet use
- found that your time on the Net takes away from or prevents you from doing other tasks and activities
- found yourself in a kind of online trance or time warp during which hours just slipped by
- frequently visited chat rooms that are focused on sexual conversation
- looked forward to your sexual activities on the Net and felt frustrated and anxious if you couldn't get on when you planned
- found yourself masturbating while on the Net
- recognized the people in the interactive online video while they recognized your screen name when you signed on
- had sexual chat-room friends who became more important than the family and friends in your life
- regularly visited porn sites
- downloaded pornography from a newsgroup
- had favorite porn sites
- visited fetish porn sites
- taken part in the CuSeeMe sexual video rooms
- viewed child pornography online

At first, discovering the Net's potential for sexual activity may have felt very exciting to you. After all, a new world was opening up for you, ready for exploration. It may have seemed like a harmless one in which to play, to fulfill fantasies, to occasionally find sexual gratification. It may have felt like a dream come true. But eventually you may have found, as have many other men and women, that cybersex has a downside—a very powerful one that is difficult, if not impossible, to control. Even as you made resolutions to limit or stop using the Net for sex, they were made hollow by the echoes of previous vows and promises. "How could this be happening to me?" you wondered. Again, you are not alone in these feelings. The power and attraction of the Internet in general, and its use for sexual activity in particular, has subtly captured countless individuals in our culture with surprising speed.

Cybersex Use Growing Rapidly

What effect has the Internet had on society since it came into use by the general public in the early 1990s? It's difficult to fully understand this now, but the speed at which it has permeated our culture is an indication of its power. As you know, sexuality is one important aspect of our lives that is being dramatically affected by the Internet. Mention "cybersex" and the response you receive will be, more often than not, a chuckle and a lewd comment. Such reactions do not, however, come from anyone who is familiar with the extent of sex on the Internet. Access to sex on the Internet is on the rise in America.

The statistics are as remarkable as they are startling:

- As of January 1999, there were 19,542,710 total unique visitors per month on the top five pay porn Web sites, and there were 98,527,275 total unique visitors per month on the top five free porn Web sites.
- In November 1999, Nielsen Net Ratings figures showed 12.5 million surfers visited porn sites in September from their homes, a 140 percent rise in traffic in just six months.
- Nearly 17 percent of Internet users have problems with using sex on the Net.
- Severe problems with sex on the Net exists for 1 percent of Internet users—and 40 percent of these extreme cases are women.
- Most e-porn traffic, about 70 percent, occurs weekdays between the hours of 9 a.m. and 5 p.m.
- There are 100,000 Web sites dedicated to selling sex in some way—this does not include chat rooms, e-mail, or other forms of sexual contact on the Web.
- About 200 sex-related Web sites are added each day.
- Sex on the Internet constitutes the third-largest economic sector on the Web (software and computers rank first and second), generating $1 billion dollars annually.
- The greatest technological innovations on the Web were developed by the sex industry (video streaming is one example).

It is easy to categorize online sexual behaviors as either all good or all bad. The Internet, however, is a powerful communications tool that is neither inherently good nor bad. It is, rather, the content offered by its creators (those who host Web sites, post to newsgroups, organize chat rooms, and so on) and the ways Internet users respond to these messages, images, and sounds that result in "good" or "bad" outcomes. Social scientists have recognized the educational potential of the Internet, citing the greater availability of information about sexuality and the potential online for more candid discussions of sexuality. The Internet also offers the opportunity for forming online, or virtual, "communities" in which isolated or disenfranchised people can communicate with one another about sexual topics.

Far more often, however, a rapidly increasing number of people find that using the Internet for sexual purposes is fraught with risks and that it interferes with many aspects of their lives, including family relationships, work life, and financial security.

Three people share their experiences here. *(Please note that while the stories used in this book are true, they have been altered as needed to protect individual anonymity.)*

Jill, a woman in her thirties:

I went online in the early evening each night. I stayed on for hours in a chat room where all the members [virtually] knew one another. These sessions became quite intense. We talked about everything in our lives, including sex, problems at home, work hassles, our vacations, just everything. And if someone was missing, then an online "crisis" occurred. Since members all had each other's phone numbers, we would call up the missing person at home to find out why he or she hadn't logged on. The conversations were sometimes sexual, but not always. The primary purpose of the chat room was connection, rather than sexual. Every time was like a conference call, but with a lot more of us online—and we were online so much that this chat room just became our life.

Saul, a young man who worked out of his home:

Beginning in 1995, I became caught up in a pattern that began each morning when, after breakfast, I would go to my computer and spend at least two hours downloading thirty-five to forty pornographic pictures and then selecting the "best" fifteen to save. This went on for more than five years. Even with a huge collection of 120 ZIP discs filled with pornographic images, I still didn't have enough. Anyway, once I had my "fifteen daily best," I would masturbate to these images. As an avid e-trader, I then turned my best efforts to making money by day-trading. I'd spend the next four or five hours playing the market, and by mid-afternoon, I was exhausted. Day in and day out, I would get up and do it all over again.

Chuck, a married corporate executive in his early fifties:

I had just sold the company I founded for a great profit. After the pressure and excitement of the months leading up to the sale, however, I felt let down and depressed. Not in the mood for much of anything, I stayed at home and began playing on the computer. One of my favorite activities was to create various personae and then advertise for dates while portraying them in online personal columns. Given the multitude of responses, I turned this into an enormously entertaining game, one that I spent hours and hours playing. Soon, days merged into nights and nights into days. Time blurred. Weeks passed unnoticed. Within a couple months, I was barely speaking to my wife and was ignoring my work completely. My life existed almost solely in cyberspace.

What Is Cybersex?

Internet sex can be accessed and experienced in many different ways. Each has the potential to cause users problems and to lead them into risky or dangerous situations. In the following section, we outline these new avenues of sex to give you an idea of the breadth of the cybersex world.

The term "cybersex" has become a catchall to describe a variety of computer based, sex-related behaviors, many of which you may recognize. They fall into three general categories:

1. Accessing Online Pornography, Audio, Video, and Text Stories

The kind of pornography available on the Internet varies widely, just as it does in the non-cyberworld, ranging from photographs of models posing in bathing suits or lingerie to young children being sexually abused. It can be found in various forms, including photos and audio, video, and text stories. Its variety and ease of access, however, is much greater than offline access. Pornographic materials can be found on personal and commercial Web pages, with access just a mouse-click away. Pornographic pictures, video, audio, and text can also be exchanged via e-mail and discussion or newsgroups. These forums allow participants to use their e-mail to post stories, ideas, photographs, or software related to the topic of the group. These messages can then be stored for other group participants to read or retrieve. Thousands of sex-related newsgroups exist on the Net and represent the highest volume of traffic of all newsgroups.

2. Real Time with a Fantasy Partner

The second form of cybersex takes place in what is known as "real time"—though time may be the only aspect of the interaction that is "real." Advanced technology has also provided ways to exchange images and files online during a live conversation. In addition, "virtual locations" exist in which you can engage in online chatting with others.

Current technology also allows for the exchange of voice and video images via the Internet. By simply providing a credit card number, you can take advantage of live video cameras that capture and transmit images of males or females engaged in everything from everyday activities to explicit sexual acts. Though a fee is common, some of these sites can be accessed for free. Some live video sites accept requests for specific sexual behaviors from online users, thus enabling an individual to create and fulfill personal fantasies. Thanks to live-video-feed technology, it is even possible to chat online while viewing pornography. Such virtual video booths are steadily growing in number and allow cybersex users to have nearly complete control over the "object" at the other end of the phone line, even though the object is a human being. For a relatively small fee, you can also link to X-rated video feeds without any interaction or, with CuSeeMe software and a Web cam, watch others masturbate or engage in other sexual activities while they watch you do the same.

3. Multimedia Software

The final category of cybersex does not take place online at all. With the invention of more sophisticated multimedia systems, people can play X-rated movies, engage in sexual games, or view the latest issues of erotic magazines on a desktop or laptop computer. Compact disc read-only memory (CD-ROM) technology allows companies to release software titles with sound and video clips. Such multimedia productions can also include erotic information.

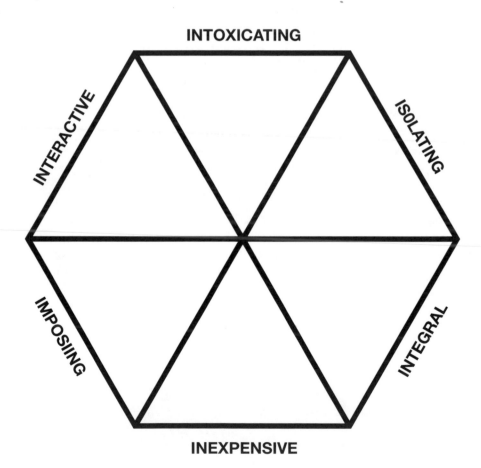

The Power of Cybersex

With all the forms of media available in our culture, what is it that attracts people to the Internet to engage in sexual activities in such a high-tech fashion? What has attracted you? We believe that the Internet has six attributes—a CyberHex—that, when taken together, make the Internet unique among all other media. The CyberHex attributes make the Internet enormously alluring for someone seeking sexual arousal and fulfillment. These six attributes are Intoxicating, Isolating, Integral, Inexpensive, Imposing, and Interactive.

Figure 1.1   **The CyberHex**

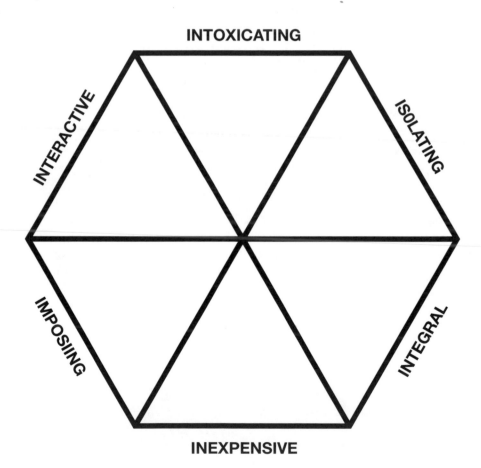

The "CyberHex" is so named not only because it is a hexagon, but also because of the altered state of mind—a trancelike state, or "hex"—that individuals report slipping into while engaging in cybersex. While any one of these six attributes can be powerful enough to entice a person into the Internet, it is often a combination of these six that draws cybersex users into a ritual of sexually acting out on the Internet. Pair these six CyberHex components with a predisposition for compulsive or addictive behavior and you have a recipe for cybersex addiction.

The Internet is the only communication medium that brings together so many attractive features. The synergy created through their interaction makes the Internet much more seductive than any other media.

It's also important to realize that the Internet CyberHex characteristics affect everyone who uses the Net, not just those who use it for sex-related reasons. This is why so many people who have no previous history of compulsive or addictive behavior are now having problems with their use of the Internet—its CyberHex spell is so powerful that people are drawn into and held in the Internet in an addictive-like way.

In her 1998 book *Caught in the Net*, author Kimberly Young explores the growing problem of Internet "addiction."[1] Her research (conducted both online and offline) showed that many survey respondents stayed online for six, eight, even ten or more hours at a time, day after day, despite the problems this habit caused in their families, their relationships, their work life, and at school. They reported feelings of anxiety and irritability when offline and craved their next opportunity to go online. Despite Internet-use-related divorces, lost jobs, or poor grades, they said they couldn't stop or even control their Internet usage. These people show typical indications of problematic Internet behavior: compulsivity, continuation despite negative consequences, and obsession. For some, it is Internet use itself that is problematic; for others, it is engaging in specific online behaviors that causes problems.

Now, let's look more closely at the Internet's six CyberHex attributes.

Intoxicating

It may seem that comparing Internet use to a drug use is absurd. Yet individuals who use the Internet for cybersex often report feeling a druglike euphoria while preparing to or engaging in cybersex. It is this "rush" that lures people back to cybersex after they have sworn off such behavior.

The Internet provides immediate access to a staggeringly immense information base. Want to read a German newspaper? No need to go to a bookstore to buy one (assuming you could find a bookstore that carried it). You need only jump online and, with a few clicks of the mouse, you are reading *Der Zietung*. It's even possible to log on to NASA's Web site at any time and access live video footage from space. No matter what our interests may be, we can easily and quickly find information about them on the Net. This immediate access plays directly into our society's demand to have desires gratified instantly. We want to get what we want immediately and everything that's available on the Internet can be reached very quickly—and not just information but communication via instant messaging, chat rooms, and e-mail.

The Internet's ease of use further adds to its seductive and intoxicating nature. Surfing the Net requires only a computer and Internet access; one can find access at home, at work, in libraries, in cybercafés, and at the homes of friends and neighbors. Need a Net "fix"? Access can be quickly at hand.

Take this inherently intoxicating nature of the Net and add to it access to sex, an obviously powerful force in people's lives, and its draw is exponentially stronger. Having the easy and immediate access the Net provides to whatever kind of sexual experiences, information, pictures, and videos you want is enormously alluring. Once online, hours can slip by unnoticed, almost as though one is in an intoxicating trance.

In addition, cybersex provides a perfect opportunity for people to develop sexual fantasies and objectify others without the fear of rejection. In fact, the CD-ROM versions of adult sexual material often let the user choose the ideal partner and ideal situation—one step beyond noninteractive magazines. Users may choose a partner's gender, age, hair color, skin color, body type, and eye color, as well as whatever sexual scenario they want to engage in. Some sexual CD-ROM titles are disguised in the form of a game. Perhaps a sexual mystery must be solved or an adventure taken in which users have to solve puzzles or find clues that lead them to their next sexual "conquest." The common factor among all cybersex material is that the user is free to become part of the fantasy without responsibility, consequence, or rejection. What's more, the variety of possibilities on the Internet is truly mind-boggling: whatever kind of sexual activity or depiction you can think of, you can likely find it on the Net.

Isolating

Perhaps the most powerful component of cybersex is isolation: the Internet allows for the aforementioned intoxication to occur quickly and privately. It provides a perfect opportunity to separate yourself from others and to engage in whatever fantasy you prefer without risk of sexually transmitted infections or the distraction of reality. Previous methods of obtaining pornography involved (at a minimum) a trip to an adult bookstore or corner market. Now, with the click of a mouse, those same images will appear on the screen with absolutely no contact with the outside world. Separated from the outside world, users can create the justifications and rationalizations needed to convince themselves and others that their behavior is both victimless and harmless.

This CyberHex attribute also exemplifies the paradoxical nature of the Internet: it can connect us to the world as never before, but, at the same time, it can separate and isolate us from others and the world as never before. While on the Internet, people have no physical contact with others. Time spent on the Net is time not spent in "real time" interactions with those who are important in our lives. A fast-growing complaint of men and women in relationships is that Net use has taken a partner away from them. The complaining partner is less and less a physical part of the using partner's life because the using partner spends so much time on the Net.

Integral

In just a few short years, the Internet has become an integral part of most people's personal and work lives. Online we can now acquire a home mortgage, shop, trade on the stock market, check the weather anywhere in the world, e=mail friends or business colleagues, create and conduct business, do research for school assignments, and so much more. The prices of computers and Internet access continue to fall and are within the range of many families. What's more, the Internet is available publicly in a variety of settings (e.g., public libraries, coffeehouses, college campuses) and simply seems to be a part of our lives. While such integration allows convenience, it also makes the Internet more difficult to avoid. The more the Internet becomes a part of our lives, the more indispensable—or "integral"—it becomes. The option to not use it becomes ever less viable.

Before the Internet's creation, access to various forms of sex-related materials and sexual experiences had limitations. Most strip clubs and XXX-rated theaters are not open twenty-four hours a day. Buying a porn magazine requires getting to a store that sells them, and most stores aren't open all the time, either. Another limitation is distance/location. Stores, theaters, strip clubs, and areas where prostitutes ply their trade cannot be conveniently found in every neighborhood of every city and suburb or rural community, thus requiring those who wish to access them to have time and transportation. The Internet changed all of this. It offers incredibly broad and easy access to sex of all kinds. Twenty-four hours a day, seven days a week, anyone with the use of a computer with an Internet connection—be it at work, a cybercafé, a public library, school, university, or in the home—can choose from literally millions of sex-related Web sites offering whatever type of sexual experience is desired.

Imposing

While related to the integral aspect of the Internet, this "imposing" attribute suggests that the role of the Internet in our lives today often goes beyond being integral. It is, in fact, becoming more and more of a necessity. Because of the extent to which the Internet is being integrated into our lives, its use is, in a sense, being externally imposed on us by society. Ironically, while the interactive nature of the Internet offers us much control over what we access, this imposing factor suggests a loss of control in that we have fewer options to decline using the Net.

To understand the difference between "integral" and "imposing," let's compare the telephone and the Internet. The telephone has long played an integral role in our lives, but it is not at all as "imposing" as the Net. While few people spend three, five, or eight hours at a time on the phone three or more times a week, many people do spend this amount of time—or more—on the Internet.

In addition, the very breath of the Internet's content is, in and of itself, formidable and imposing. While choice may be good in many circumstances, having too much from which to choose can be overwhelming. Think of the Internet as a Thanksgiving dinner gone wild. There are so many enticing "dishes" and "desserts" from which to choose that you want to sample every one. You know that if you do, however, you'll feel awful afterward. It's hard to say, "No," and despite our best efforts at control, we often overindulge. The Internet offers us so many enticing opportunities that it's difficult to decline. Soon, some people find themselves overindulging to the detriment of their health, families, relationships, and work. And still, stopping seems impossible.

Interactive

Unlike other forms of media, the Internet is truly interactive. Shout or cajole as we might at the faces on our TV screen or at the writer of a magazine or newspaper editorial, we'll get no response. The Internet, however, lets us truly interact with others. We guide it to the locations, people, and information of our choice. Some interactive sex sites allow viewers to choose the person they want to interact with and the activity that will take place. With the right equipment and software, conversations can be in real time. The Internet gives us a sense of control over what we see and receive.

Inexpensive

For anyone on a budget, cybersex provides a low-cost means to a sexual high. Hard-core pornography magazines may run fifteen to fifty dollars. However, for the cost of Internet access (ten to twenty-five dollars per month), anyone can find hundreds of photographs, stories, chat channels, and more. In addition, the user can choose to retrieve and view only the information that is of interest; there's no need to purchase an entire magazine full of mostly unwanted advertisements and articles.

Sex on the Internet: what you want, when you want it, at low cost, minus the messiness and hassles of a real person-to-person relationship, and with complete anonymity. It should not be surprising that the number of sex-related Web sites is exploding, along with the number of people accessing and using them.

These six CyberHex factors also seem to increase the chances that the Internet will become a problem for those who already struggle with sexual compulsivity and for those who are emotionally or psychologically vulnerable to such sexual availability.

While research in the area of cybersex usage is only beginning, a recent survey by Al Cooper, David Delmonico, and Ron Burg of 9,265 Internet users describes three categories of people who use the Internet for sexual pursuits:[2]

- Recreational users are people who access online sexual material more out of curiosity or for entertainment purposes and are not typically seen as having problems associated with their online sexual behaviors.

- At-risk users may never have developed a problem with online sexuality if not for the availability of the Internet. These individuals use the Internet a moderate amount of time for sexual activities, and, if their pattern of use continues and increases, they could become compulsive.

- Sexually compulsive users are those who, due to a propensity for pathological sexual expression, use the Internet as a forum for their sexual activities. For this group in particular, the power of isolation, fantasy, anonymity, and affordability interacts with certain underlying personality factors to increase their use of the Internet for sexual activities to the point where it becomes difficult, if not impossible, for them to control. Remember that compulsion is a sign of an addictive disorder. One of the signs of addiction to alcohol or another drug is that the substance is used compulsively.

The study found that while 84 percent of the respondents did not meet the criteria for cybersex compulsivity, 6 percent of all respondents scored in a way that suggested cybersex compulsivity. A third group of approximately 10 percent of the entire sample also emerged as "at-risk" users who may not be exhibiting all signs of cybersex compulsion but who are in a potentially dangerous stage with their behavior. According to a July 2000 Nielsen survey, there are 148.8 million Internet users in the United States alone. (International Data Corporation reports that total worldwide Internet users exceed 200 million.) Extrapolating from the cybersex use percentages in the study by Cooper, Delmonico, and Burg, approximately 8.9 million people in the United States (6 percent of 148.8 million) need intervention for their compulsive use of cybersex. In addition, there are another 14.8 million individuals (10 percent of 148.8 million) who are using cybersex moderately and show beginning signs of sexual compulsivity. Their continued use can predictably be a significant danger to many of them. Unfortunately, researchers are concerned that these approximations may be extremely conservative estimates.

Exercise 1: What Attracts You to the Internet?

Now that we've discussed the Internet's CyberHex, we would like you to think about these six characteristics—Intoxicating, Isolating, Integral, Imposing, Interactive, and Inexpensive—and the influence they have on you.

In the chart below, first list these six characteristics, beginning at the top with the one that is most appealing to you and ending with the one that is least attractive.

Next, in the right-hand column, list all the ways this particular CyberHex characteristic pulls you into the Net. What is its "hook" for you? Please take your time and be as thorough as you can. In chapter 4, we will ask you to refer to the information you've written here.

CHARACTERISTIC	WHY IT'S ATTRACTIVE
1. Intoxicating	Easy / Quick
2. Isolating	Private, low risk of getting caught

CHARACTERISTIC	WHY IT'S ATTRACTIVE
3. Integral	Way to reduce stress (self soothing)
4. Inexpensible	cheaper than Videos
5. Imposing	Didnt feel it was imposing
6. Interactive	Didnt use it in an interactive way

In Conclusion

There is little doubt that use of the Internet will continue to explode. As people spend more time online and look to the Internet to fulfill an ever increasing number of their sexual needs and fantasies, the problems associated with online sexuality will increase proportionately.

We have written this workbook to help you better understand how problematic Internet sexual behavior begins, increases in strength, and even becomes addictive. More important, it also provides a step-by-step plan for successfully dealing with problematic cybersex activities that can enable you to regain control of your life and your relationships. There is help and hope here for anyone who feels entangled in the web of cybersex.

In this chapter, we've explained how cybersex can hold so much power over people's lives. The above exercise helped you begin to think more about your use of the Internet for sexual purposes. In the next chapter, you will learn more about the five types of cybersex users, the indicators of problematic cybersex usage, and the ten criteria of problematic online sexual behavior.

CHAPTER 2: *Understanding Problematic Cybersex Behavior*

In this chapter, we will look at the types of problematic online sexual behavior, and we'll show you how that behavior can become so compulsive that it seems impossible to control.

It's important to note that not everyone who uses the Internet for sexual activities does so for the same reason or to the same extent, and that not all cybersex has negative consequences. We have divided those who are engaging in sexual behavior on the Internet into five groups, illustrated by the diagram in figure 1 below.

Figure 1

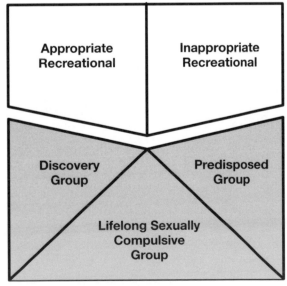

Recreational Cybersex Users

Recreational cybersex users can be divided into two categories: appropriate recreational users and inappropriate recreational users. The former seem to be able to explore sex on the Internet without any sign of their behavior becoming problematic. Their behavior is out in the open, not covert. Time spent in cybersex behaviors is minimal, usually totaling no more than a couple of hours a week. They do not feel embarrassed or shameful about these activities, and often they take part in them with their spouse or partner. They may, in fact, use cybersex as a way to enhance their sexual experience with one another and thus to strengthen their relationship.

The latter group of recreational cybersex users includes individuals who do not have a compulsive or addictive problem with sex on the Internet, but who use what they find on the Net inappropriately. They may, for example, show a sex-related item or site they discovered on the Net to others such as their work colleagues, family members, or friends who are not interested in such information or who are embarrassed by it. They do so not as a means of hurting or embarrassing others, but simply because they think such information is funny or because they like the feeling of shocking others. These individuals who use cybersex inappropriately don't try to hide their activities either, whereas people who have a more serious problem with cybersex go to great lengths to cover up their cybersex activities from others in their lives.

Problematic Cybersex Users

People who exhibit problematic sexual behavior on the Internet tend to fall into one of three groups:

1. **Discovery Group**: those who have no previous problem with online sex or any history of problematic sexual behavior

2. **Predisposed Group**: those who have had their first out-of-control sexual behavior on the Internet while obsessing over unacted-on sexual fantasies and urges

3. **Lifelong Sexually Compulsive Group**: those whose out-of-control sexual behavior on the Internet is part of an ongoing and severe sexual behavior problem

Discovery Group

People in this group have no previous problem with online sex and no history of problematic sexual behavior. Debra's story is typical of this group:

In my early twenties, I hadn't had much of a sex life. Not only had I never even had a sexual relationship, I'd hardly ever kissed anyone. It wasn't that I didn't have an interest in men. I just felt uncomfortable approaching and meeting eligible guys.

One day while surfing the Net, I discovered that there were sex-related sites. I guess I'd just never imagined that this kind of thing would be on the Internet. Well, I was totally overwhelmed. For the first time in my life, I could explore relationships and my sexuality. I was soon spending countless hours online visiting sexually oriented chat rooms and writing ads for the online personal columns. I discovered that I was attracted to men from other countries. After conversing online with a number of them, I finally decided to meet one guy who seemed pretty special for a ten-day tour in France. How did it turn out? The tour was fine, but the guy was anything but. He was crude, physically not at all how he'd described himself, and he had the personality of a doorknob. I've met a few other men this way, too, and I've always been disappointed, but I haven't given up. I'm sure I'll find "Mr. Right" eventually.

There is, in a sense, a healthy aspect to Debra's story in that she had wanted to have sexual relationships and the Internet freed her to do so. She discovered and explored her ideas about relationships and sexuality through the Internet. On the other hand, Debra became completely carried away with her online activities, spending many hours at her computer. By courting and meeting strangers about whom she actually knew very little, Debra also put herself in great danger. A wiser and safer choice for her would be to use one of the many available dating services that carefully screen their members.

Predisposed Group

This group is made up of people who have never acted out sexually—though they have thought about it—until they discovered cybersex. They might have fantasized about exposing themselves or had the urge to see a prostitute or go to a strip club. Until they discovered the world of cybersex, however, they were able to control their fantasies and urges. Maybe they were afraid of being recognized at a strip club or being arrested in a prostitution sting. Perhaps they simply were healthy enough and possessed adequate coping skills to recognize and resist these impulses.

People in this group may not use the Net for sexual purposes as frequently as people in some of the other groups, but they are certainly at risk for more problematic online sexual behavior. With the Internet, sex is just a mouse-click away, and at some point, they discover sexually explicit activities that they just can't resist. At first, the consequences of their cybersex activities may seem minimal. After all, no one will see them or recognize them online.

Katie's story is an excellent example of this behavior:

I had often wondered what it would be like to have sex with another woman. I was twenty-eight, happily married with two children. For a few years, I'd heard more about bisexuality and began to realize that I might be bisexual. I didn't know how to explain that while sex with my husband was great, I still had sexual feelings for some women, too. I was getting more interested, but I'd always been a little afraid to act on these feelings, and besides, I didn't know, really, how I could go about meeting a woman who felt the same as I did. Besides, I wasn't interested just in sex. I wanted a real relationship in which there would be a sense of connection, too. Since I'd occasionally visited chat rooms in the past, one night I decided to search for one focused on lesbianism. To my surprise, I found lots of such sites. I was instantly intrigued and soon began spending more time online in lesbian-oriented chat rooms. While these online activities were positive experiences at first that helped me sort out my feelings, I began to spend so much time online that other aspects of my life started to suffer. I was tired from staying up too late at night, and so I had less time and energy for my family and work. In fact, my supervisor actually had a talk with me in which he wanted to know if something was wrong in my life because I'd been having trouble meeting deadlines.

Paul's story is also typical of people in this group:

After nine years of marriage, I'd never been unfaithful to my wife. Had I had opportunities? Sure, but I never acted on them because I felt it was wrong. The last couple of years, however, I had spent a lot of time fantasizing about having an affair because things weren't going so well in my marriage. Almost by chance, I found a chat room in which there were others like me with similar feelings about their relationships. One day—well, actually it was about 2:00 in the morning—I began conversing with a woman and soon found that we had much in common. Our conversations were fun, interesting, and progressively more sexual. I loved how I felt after my time online with her—energized, excited, supported, and satisfied. Eventually, we began having sex online. Was I being unfaithful? I decided I wasn't because I wasn't really having actual sex with anyone. We'd never met and I didn't even know her real name. Eventually she suggested we meet in person at a hotel for dinner and sex—which we did. I'd broken the promise I'd made to myself and the scary thing about it was that it had all been so easy—easy to arrange to meet her online, easy to meet her in person, and easy to have sex with her. Soon I became involved with other women, too.

Part of the power of cybersex is that it's one step removed from reality. Having thoughts, urges, and fantasies and then acting on them via the Internet seems different from acting on them in the physical world. On the Net, we are not face-to-face, literally, with another human being. We can't look into their eyes, feel their touch, read their emotions, or in any other way physically interact with them. Cyber-interactions feel more remote, safer. The "other" is out there somewhere, at arm's length. Our computer and the Net feel like some kind of magical place where everything is safe and secure. We can be whoever we want to be, with no apparent consequences.

This distance, however, also makes it easier to cross behavior lines that we would not otherwise violate—something that's not uncommon for people in this group. Paul, for example, swore he'd never have an affair, but that is exactly what he was doing, albeit initially without actual physical contact. People in this group often have clear boundaries for their urges or fantasies—until they encounter the cyber-world, where they feel okay about pushing beyond them. Once that boundary is stretched or breached, little may be left to control behavior.

Lifelong Sexually Compulsive Group

People in this group have been involved in problematic sexual behavior throughout most of their lives. They might compulsively masturbate, compulsively use pornography, practice voyeurism or exhibitionism, or compulsively frequent strip clubs and prostitutes. For these people, cybersex simply provides a new option for acting out sexually that fits within their already existing patterns of problematic behavior.

Karl's story is typical of people in this group:

> As a child, I was sexually abusive to my younger sister. During adolescence, I frequently exposed myself to others. This behavior began as a bit of a joke at first. I would "streak" a sporting event or beach, for example. By this time in my life, I had already been molesting children, but in a less obvious manner. I'd try to get young girls to sit on my lap and then fondle them—but always under the pretext of trying to help them off my lap. As a young adult, I got arrested for exposing myself to teenage girls.
>
> I discovered online sex before most people had even heard of the Internet, because I did a lot of computer programming. I looked at a lot of porn online at work since I couldn't have magazines like that lying around my office. I spent hours each day in nudist, exhibitionist, and voyeur sex sites, with a particular preference for nudist sites with pictures of children.
>
> After cybersex became better known, some of my employers installed monitoring equipment to stop people from looking at sex sites, but that was never a problem for me because I was able to thwart any site blockouts or attempts by my company's tech information services staff to monitor my online behavior. The truth was that I used cybersex merely as a stopgap measure while I was at work because I didn't dare expose myself there. I finally had to enter treatment after I was arrested for exposing myself to two girls at a health-club swimming pool.

Karl's story shows the intensity of what it's like to have an out-of-control sexual behavior and how it is fueled by accessing online sexually oriented Internet sites.

There are three separate cybersex subgroups within the lifelong sexually compulsive group. First, there are those people who use the Internet as an additional way of acting out with the same behaviors they use offline. Someone like Karl, who exposes himself regularly, can do so now on the Net (using a Web cam) with far less risk than doing so in public.

A second group of people includes those who see the Internet as a less risky way of acting out. One client of ours, whom we'll call Samuel, enjoyed frequenting strip clubs and hustling young women in bars. The Internet offered him the opportunity to view live video feeds from strip clubs, and thanks to online chat rooms, he could spend time in teen-oriented rooms talking with young girls whenever he wanted. As long as he didn't try to meet them, he felt his behavior was safe and acceptable. Cybersex allows people in this group to feed their compulsion in virtual anonymity and to receive the high from this behavior with less risk than if they were interacting face-to-face with someone.

The final group includes people whose sexual behavior is out of control already and who use the Internet to further increase the danger associated with their sexual behavior.

Our client, Samuel, discovered that his fascination with preadolescent girls increased after spending so much time in teen chat rooms:

> Soon, I found myself driving past school yards during recess and by playgrounds on summer weekends, but I never went so far as to risk actually talking to any girls. I'd stop and park, and then just fantasize about picking up one of the young girls, talking to her, and fondling her. Through the Internet, I could easily have these personal conversations with young girls. By doing this, I had really crossed a line into more dangerous territory, but that just made me more turned on and excited because I was actually doing what I had been afraid to do for so many years.

Do I Have a Problem with Cybersex?

Now we will help you look more closely at your use of sexually explicit material on the Internet. You may have many questions about when or even if using the Internet for sex is a real problem. By reading the stories of others, you'll be able to look more closely at your own Internet behavior and determine whether it's a problem.

In chapter 1, we looked at the many ways people use the Internet for sex. Reading about these people may have left you wondering about how you and others view your use of the Internet. You might now be asking yourself, "Do I have a problem with my sexual use of the Internet?" "How would I know if there's a problem?" "Am I at risk for sexually problematic behavior on the Internet?" or "Just what is 'problematic' sexual behavior on the Internet?"

First, let's clarify our use of the word "problematic." When a particular behavior or a set of behaviors begins to interfere with other aspects of your life, psychologists, psychiatrists, and counselors call them problematic. This simply means that these behaviors are causing problems and jeopardizing important areas in your life. Let's say, for example, that you've been using the Internet for sex more than ever lately. You've gone online with the intention of staying there for thirty minutes only to suddenly realize that two or three hours have slipped by. On more than one occasion, this "slipup" had some consequence—once you missed an important business appointment and another time you were late picking up your daughter from soccer. Perhaps you learned of some consequence only later. It's not unusual for people to be unaware of the consequence their actions are having in their own and in other people's lives.

When isolated instances like this occur, they probably are not an indication of a problem. However, if they continue or increase, it may be a signal to pay more attention to what is happening. As these behaviors expand and we become aware of them, we may try to avoid or minimize consequences by attempting to control the problematic behavior. Unfortunately, during this time it also becomes more difficult to see what is happening and to control our behaviors.

Indicators of Problematic Behavior

Three criteria are often used as indicators of problematic behavior. They are compulsivity, continuation despite adverse consequences, and obsession.[1] Here are explanations of each:

Compulsivity

This means the loss of the ability to choose = whether to stop a behavior. In our daily lives, we establish habit-forming routines. We often get up at the same time every day, brush our teeth in the same way, keep a work area arranged in a particular order, put the same arm into a shirt first when getting dressed, and shop at the same grocery store week after week. We repeat many behaviors, often to the point where they become habits. Habits serve a useful function in that they free us from having to actually think about what we're doing all the time. Imagine how difficult it would be if every single time you began to put on your shirt or brush your teeth, you had to think about how to do these tasks.

Compulsive behavior, however, is altogether different from routine habits. It is out-of-control behavior marked by deeply entangled rituals and obsessions, along with overwhelming feelings of frustration, self-blame, powerlessness, and hopelessness. Gerry experienced these feelings and shares his story about what life is like when using cybersex compulsively:

> *Here I was, in my early fifties, my children grown and out of the house, unhappy in my marriage, and dissatisfied with my job. I felt that, given my age, I should have had more responsibility and been making more money in my career, but that didn't seem to be happening. I had long fantasized about having an affair with a younger woman but had never followed through because I was worried about being found out by someone I knew. I knew I would die of embarrassment if my wife or friends found out. One day at home, I was surfing porn sites when I discovered a link to a site that offered live video feeds from a strip club—twenty-four hours a day, no less! Here was the answer to my dreams. If I couldn't date a younger woman, at least I could have something more tangible to feed my fantasy.*
>
> *That first time, I stayed online for a couple hours . . . until I heard the garage door opening when my wife and some friends arrived home. Forced to quickly jump offline, I was already wondering when I could find a way to get back to that site.*

I found myself visiting this and other strip club sites more and more often. Gradually, my Internet use increased from thirty minutes to an hour, then to two hours or more every night. I began spending fifteen to twenty hours a week online, surfing porn sites. I was staying up at night more and more often. I was on these sites more and more often at work, and for longer periods of time. Finally, I made a promise to myself that I'd set some rules for my use. I made a commitment to stop doing this at work and to visit porn sites at home only every other day for thirty minutes.

That promise was broken after only a week or so. I rationalized by saying, "Well, no one else is at home, so what difference does it make?" Cybersex became an obsession for me. I just couldn't stay away from it.

Continuation Despite Adverse Consequences

It is common to continue compulsive behavior despite adverse consequences, such as loss of health, job, relationships, marriage, or freedom. All behaviors have consequences—some positive and some negative. At a relatively basic level, if we brush and floss our teeth regularly, we'll have a more positive experience at the dental office. If we neglect our teeth, the consequences will include painful dental procedures and costly dental bills. We learn how to work cooperatively and meet expectations on the job, thus avoiding being fired.

Most of the time, we are able to look at our behavior and make the appropriate changes to reduce negative consequences. Unfortunately, when compulsive behavior is involved, this isn't the case.

At first, Gerry didn't see any negative consequences resulting from his Internet use, but it was only a matter of time before he was discovered.

One weekend afternoon my wife was having lunch with her sister. Not expecting her home for a couple more hours, I was completely occupied by a teen chat room I'd just discovered. I hadn't ever been in a chat room before and was amazed at what I'd found. I pretended to be another teen, commenting occasionally just so no one in the room would become suspicious. Slowly I realized that this might be a way to meet a teenage girl, my ultimate fantasy. I never heard my wife's car pull up in the driveway or the door to the house open. Walking into my office, my wife inadvertently glanced at the computer screen, only to read some rather sexual text. "Gerry, what are you doing? What's this all about? How long has this been going on? And why?"

I made up a string of apologies and promised to behave myself in the future. I didn't dare visit the strip clubs or chat rooms at home anymore. Instead, I began spending more time at work visiting sexually explicit sites. One day, however, a company memo was circulated warning all employees that our Internet usage was now being monitored during work hours and that visiting porn sites was expressly forbidden. I knew that the company was serious. In fact, I'd heard of another employee who'd been caught surfing porn sites and who was warned that if he did it again, he'd be fired on the spot.

Realizing I'd better be careful, I decided that I'd only go to the chat rooms, and only before or after hours when almost no one was around. Plus, I'd only stay online for ten or fifteen minutes. I convinced myself that I wouldn't really be violating company policy if I wasn't at an actual porn site. After a week, I found this regimen too difficult and began to log on to the chat rooms during work hours. I started believing that visiting during my lunch hour would be safe. I also thought that by now enough time had passed since my wife discovered my computer activity, so it was okay to start going to these sites again on my home computer, too, as long as I was careful.

Despite Gerry's attempts at control and the potentially dire consequences, he continued his behavior and no longer thought about how he could stop it. Instead, he tried to find a way to visit sex-related sites without incurring any negative consequences. Gerry's behavior had both direct and indirect negative consequences—though he was not immediately aware of all of them. By calculating the number of hours he spent on these sites at work and multiplying that number by his hourly wage, it is easy to see that his employer was losing thousands of dollars in productivity. What might—or should—Gerry have accomplished for his company in the hours he was "missing" at work?

Obsession

Obsession means being so preoccupied, you focus exclusively on a particular behavior (in this case, sex) to the exclusion of other parts of your life and without care for the consequences of that behavior. You are obsessed with something when you just can't stop thinking about it. It occupies much of your mental energy most of the time. In our example, Gerry had become obsessed with his use of the Internet to visit particular Web sites.

By this point, Gerry really lived in one of three states of mind: planning his next visit to an online strip club or teen chat room, being online, and coming down from a visit. In one way or another, these sites were always on his mind. When he was at work in a meeting, for example, Gerry was thinking about how long the meeting was going to last. He was trying to figure out whether he'd have ten minutes or so during a break to go online.

You might be wondering what eventually happened to Gerry.

I spent more time in the chat rooms and eventually found a young girl who agreed to meet me. Well, the "girl" wasn't a girl, as it turned out, but rather an adult male FBI agent running a sting operation. After my arrest, I admitted that I knew the "girl" I was trying to meet was under eighteen, but I was so flattered by the thought of

Exercise 1: Creating an Internet Activity Log

her wanting to meet me that I arranged the rendezvous anyway. I knew I was taking a chance but just couldn't stop myself.

Before you can decide how to change your online behaviors, it's important to know exactly what they are. To do this, we are going to ask you to keep a log of all your online activity (not just your cybersex activity) for one week. Include time online at all locations where you use a computer: home, work, cybercafé, library, or school. Don't be concerned about changing your behavior at the moment; just record it. To help you do this, use the chart below. Please be honest and accurate, because the information you gather here will be important in upcoming exercises and tasks.

Date: _Some Time in April 2003_   **Time logged on to the Net:** _12:30/1:00 am_

Site visited: _www.jennamay.com_   **What type of site:** _XXX porn_

Where was the computer you used to access the Net? (Home? Work?) _____
Describe:

Home, downstairs

_____

Why did you go to this site?

To Masturbate

_____

_____

_____

What did you do while at this site?

Masterbated to on-demand videos

_____

_____

Describe your feelings while at this site:

Felt bad that I was doing it, but also felt that I deserved to masterbate since my partner was not interested in having sex with me.

Time spent at this site: 10 minutes

Site visited: _____   What type of site: _____

Where was the computer you used to access the Net? (Home? Work?) _____
Describe:

Why did you go to this site?

What did you do while at this site?

_____

_____

_____

_____

_____

Describe your feelings while at this site:

_____

_____

_____

_____

Time spent at this site:_____

Site visited: _____   **What type of site:** _____

Where was the computer you used to access the Net? (Home? Work?) _____
Describe:

_____

_____

Why did you go to this site?

_____

_____

_____

_____

What did you do while at this site?

_____

_____

_____

_____

Describe your feelings while at this site:

_____

_____

_____

_____

Time spent at this site:_____

Time you logged off the Net: _____   **Total time online:** _____

Date: _____   **Time logged on to the Net:** _____

Site visited: _____   **What type of site:** _____

Where was the computer you used to access the Net? (Home? Work?) _____
Describe:

_____

_____

Why did you go to this site?

_____

_____

_____

_____

What did you do while at this site?

_____

_____

_____

_____

Describe your feelings while at this site:

_____

_____

_____

_____

Time spent at this site:_____

Site visited: _____   **What type of site:** _____

Where was the computer you used to access the Net? (Home? Work?) _____
Describe:

_____

_____

Why did you go to this site?

_____

_____

_____

_____

What did you do while at this site?

_____

_____

_____

_____

_____

Describe your feelings while at this site:

_____

_____

_____

_____

Time spent at this site:_____

Site visited: _____   **What type of site:** _____

Where was the computer you used to access the Net? (Home? Work?) _____
Describe:

_____

_____

Why did you go to this site?

_____

_____

_____

_____

What did you do while at this site?

_____

_____

_____

_____

_____

Describe your feelings while at this site:

_____

_____

_____

_____

Time spent at this site:_____

Time you logged off the Net: _____   **Total time online:** _____

Date: _____   **Time logged on to the Net:** _____

Site visited: _____   **What type of site:** _____

Where was the computer you used to access the Net? (Home? Work?) _____
Describe:

_____

_____

Why did you go to this site?

_____

_____

_____

_____

What did you do while at this site?

_____

_____

_____

_____

Describe your feelings while at this site:

_____

_____

_____

_____

Time spent at this site:_____

Site visited: _____   **What type of site:** _____

Where was the computer you used to access the Net? (Home? Work?) _____
Describe:

_____

_____

Why did you go to this site?

_____

_____

_____

_____

What did you do while at this site?

_____

_____

_____

_____

_____

Describe your feelings while at this site:

_____

_____

_____

_____

Time spent at this site:_____

Site visited: _____   **What type of site:** _____

Where was the computer you used to access the Net? (Home? Work?) _____
Describe:

_____

_____

Why did you go to this site?

_____

_____

_____

_____

What did you do while at this site?

_____

_____

_____

_____

Describe your feelings while at this site:

_____

_____

_____

_____

Time spent at this site:_____

Time you logged off the Net: _____   **Total time online:** _____

Date: _____   Time logged on to the Net:_____

Site visited: _____   What type of site: _____

Where was the computer you used to access the Net? (Home? Work?) _____
Describe:

_____

_____

Why did you go to this site?

_____

_____

_____

_____

What did you do while at this site?

_____

_____

_____

_____

Describe your feelings while at this site:

_____

_____

_____

_____

Time spent at this site:_____

Site visited: _____   **What type of site:** _____

Where was the computer you used to access the Net? (Home? Work?) _____
Describe:

_____

_____

Why did you go to this site?

_____

_____

_____

_____

What did you do while at this site?

_____

_____

_____

_____

_____

Describe your feelings while at this site:

_____

_____

_____

_____

Time spent at this site:_____

Site visited: _____ **What type of site:** _____

Where was the computer you used to access the Net? (Home? Work?) _____
Describe:

_____

_____

Why did you go to this site?

_____

_____

_____

_____

What did you do while at this site?

_____

_____

_____

_____

_____

Describe your feelings while at this site:

_____

_____

_____

_____

Time spent at this site:_____

Time you logged off the Net: _____   **Total time online:** _____

Date: _____   **Time logged on to the Net:** _____

Site visited: _____   **What type of site:** _____

Where was the computer you used to access the Net? (Home? Work?) _____
Describe:

_____

_____

Why did you go to this site?

_____

_____

_____

_____

What did you do while at this site?

_____

_____

_____

_____

Describe your feelings while at this site:

_____

_____

_____

_____

Time spent at this site:_____

Site visited: _____   **What type of site:** _____

Where was the computer you used to access the Net? (Home? Work?) _____
Describe:

_____

_____

Why did you go to this site?

_____

_____

_____

_____

What did you do while at this site?

_____

_____

_____

_____

_____

Describe your feelings while at this site:

_____

_____

_____

_____

Time spent at this site:_____

Site visited: _____ **What type of site:** _____

Where was the computer you used to access the Net? (Home? Work?) _____
Describe:

_____

_____

Why did you go to this site?

_____

_____

_____

_____

What did you do while at this site?

_____

_____

_____

_____

Describe your feelings while at this site:

_____

_____

_____

_____

Time spent at this site:_____

Time you logged off the Net: _____   **Total time online:** _____

Date: _____ **Time logged on to the Net:**_____

Site visited: _____ **What type of site:** _____

Where was the computer you used to access the Net? (Home? Work?) _____
Describe:

_____

_____

Why did you go to this site?

_____

_____

_____

_____

What did you do while at this site?

_____

_____

_____

_____

Describe your feelings while at this site:

_____

_____

_____

_____

Time spent at this site:_____

Site visited: _____   **What type of site:** _____

Where was the computer you used to access the Net? (Home? Work?) _____
Describe:

_____

_____

Why did you go to this site?

_____

_____

_____

_____

What did you do while at this site?

_____

_____

_____

_____

_____

Describe your feelings while at this site:

_____

_____

_____

_____

Time spent at this site:_____

Site visited: _____   **What type of site:** _____

Where was the computer you used to access the Net? (Home? Work?) _____
Describe:

_____

_____

Why did you go to this site?

_____

_____

_____

_____

What did you do while at this site?

_____

_____

_____

_____

Describe your feelings while at this site:

_____

_____

_____

_____

Time spent at this site:_____

Time you logged off the Net: _____   **Total time online:** _____

Date: _____   **Time logged on to the Net:**_____

Site visited: _____   **What type of site:** _____

Where was the computer you used to access the Net? (Home? Work?) _____
Describe:

_____

_____

Why did you go to this site?

_____

_____

_____

_____

What did you do while at this site?

_____

_____

_____

_____

Describe your feelings while at this site:

_____

_____

_____

_____

Time spent at this site:_____

Site visited: _____   **What type of site:** _____

Where was the computer you used to access the Net? (Home? Work?) _____
Describe:

_____

_____

Why did you go to this site?

_____

_____

_____

_____

What did you do while at this site?

_____

_____

_____

_____

_____

Describe your feelings while at this site:

_____

_____

_____

_____

Time spent at this site:_____

Site visited: _____ **What type of site:** _____

Where was the computer you used to access the Net? (Home? Work?) _____
Describe:

_____

_____

Why did you go to this site?

_____

_____

_____

_____

What did you do while at this site?

_____

_____

_____

_____

_____

Describe your feelings while at this site:

_____

_____

_____

_____

Time spent at this site:_____

Time you logged off the Net: _____   **Total time online:** _____

Exercise 2: Ten Criteria of Problematic Online Sexual Behavior

Previously, we talked about how difficult it is to determine whether a given online sexual behavior is actually problematic. Taking into consideration Gerry's account of his online sexual behavior, do you think he has a problem?

To help you evaluate your own online sexual behavior, we've developed the following set of ten criteria of problematic online sexual behavior. After reading each one, you will find a series of questions. Please answer them as honestly and thoroughly as you can in the space provided. If a criteria or question does not apply to you, make a note of this.

1. Preoccupation with Sex on the Internet

This is more than just thinking about online sex; it means that you have some difficulty not thinking about it. You may think about cybersex a lot, but not all the time. Sometimes, when you're in a meeting or having a conversation or at a play or sporting event, you're engrossed in the moment. You think about sex during those sorts of activities only some of the time. Mostly, you think about cybersex a lot in your spare time. At *some* level, however, these thoughts are always with you. You find yourself regularly wondering how you can orchestrate your life in ways that will allow you time online. You think about past online sexual experiences or about what future online experiences will be like. Sometimes you find it difficult to get away from thoughts about online sex. You may even find yourself dreaming about sex on the Internet. It's there in both your conscious and unconscious minds.

Do you structure your day to be sure there's time for online sex? If so, describe.

_no_

How often do you do this?

1/2 week ~ 1/2 month

Do you look forward to your time online for cybersex? If so, describe when and how this happens.

No., i feel its a last resort.

2. Engaging in sex on the Internet More Often or for Longer Periods of Time Than Intended

When you look at the amount of time you're spending online, you see that it has been increasing. You decided, for example, to go online for sex for just an hour, but when you looked at the clock, you realized you'd been on for more than two hours. You don't know where the time went. Perhaps you told yourself you could be online for just two hours from midnight to 2:00 a.m., but suddenly you discover you've been online until 4:00 a.m. You had originally been going online for sex-related activities a couple days a week. Now you're on daily, and not just once, but four, five, six, or more times per day. You keep track of your time for a few days and discover that you're actually spending five hours a day online for sex-related activities.

In a sense, you are developing a "tolerance" to Internet usage. The concept of tolerance is common in the field of drug and alcohol addiction. When people begin drinking, for example, they may feel intoxicated after only one or two beers. Over time, however, their bodies develop a tolerance to alcohol and they find that they need six, eight, or twelve bottles of beer to achieve that same high. The concept applies to Internet sex, too. Many people have discovered that they have a psychological need to be online more and more over time to achieve the same high.

Has the time you spend on the Net for cybersex increased? If so, describe how it's changed over the last few months. Be specific. Also describe when and where you do cybersex.

No.

3. Repeated Unsuccessful Efforts to Control, Cut Back on, or Stop Engaging in Sex on the Internet

Once you realized that the amount of time you'd been spending for sex online was excessive, you decided to set some limits. Perhaps you promised yourself that you would go online only once a day or twice a week and only for thirty minutes at a time. Or maybe you decided to quit altogether for one week or to go online only on weekends. But whatever promise you made to yourself, you couldn't keep it. Your attempts at control may have worked for a while, but eventually, something happened and you "needed" to go back online. No matter what you tried, you eventually returned to the Internet for sexual activities.

If you've tried to cut back on your cybersex activities, describe how you've done so and what the results of your efforts have been. If you've tried to do this more than once, describe your other attempts, too.

Decided to stop after getting married

4. Restlessness or Irritability When Attempting to Limit or Stop Engaging in Sex on the Internet

When you've attempted to stop or limit your online sexual activity, you find that you become nervous and irritable. If you haven't noticed this yourself, think about what others who know you—family members, friends, work colleagues—would say if you asked them about this. Often, these people will recognize changes in your behavior before you yourself can see them. Do you know someone who has recently quit smoking? If so, how did this person act in the first days and weeks without a cigarette?

If you've tried to limit or stop your cybersex activities, how did you feel and act when you did so?

I would get frustrated mad if I wasn't sexual every week. After about a month, I decided it was ok if I masterbated

The only way I thought I could do that is
with porn.

_____

_____

_____

_____

_____

_____

5. Using Sex on the Internet as a Way of Escaping from Problems or Relieving Feelings such as Helplessness, Guilt, Anxiety, or Depression

Everyone has feelings of helplessness, sorrow, worry, depression, and anger. There are many ways to address and cope with these feelings.

When you are feeling down and would like a little boost, do you turn to the Internet for a sexual release so you can feel better? If so, please describe two of these times.

Yes. This is my motivation for every time I was
on the internet porn altes. Once was after not having
sex, another time was when I couldn't sleep

_____

_____

_____

Do you use cybersex as a way of escaping from problems or relieving feelings? If so, please describe.

Yes. I use it as a way of dealing (releasing) stress
or avoiding conflict

_____

_____

_____

_____

_____

6. Returning to Sex on the Internet Day after Day in Search of a More Intense or Higher-Risk Sexual Experience

Your expectations of what you want out of the Internet continue to increase and become more elaborate. You might hope to find your true love via the Internet. At first, you may drop into chat rooms, remaining anonymous, just to see whether you could find a potential mate online. Being anonymous no longer does it for you. Your search of various chat rooms becomes more intense, frantic, and time-consuming. After connecting with one man in particular, you begin corresponding privately with him via e-mail. Eventually, you arrange a meeting with him for sex in a hotel. The excitement and hope you feel in your search leads to more risky behavior both on and off the Internet.

What have you been looking for sexually on the Internet?

Videos, naughty women that w/ women _____

_____

_____

_____

How has that changed from when you first started going online for sex?

_No_ _____

_____

_____

Are you moving into areas you once told yourself you'd never explore? If so, what are they? How do you feel about this change?

_No._

7. Lying to Family Members, Therapists, or Others to Conceal Involvement With Sex on the Internet

In our culture, most people are secretive about their sex lives, regardless of whether their behavior is normal or problematic. What is of concern is being dishonest about it when asked. When one of our clients was questioned by his wife about his late nights on the computer, he regularly answered by saying that it was a work-related project with a tight deadline. When initially confronted about his use of the Internet for sexual purposes, Gerry lied to his wife about his behavior.

Have you lied about using the Internet for sex-related activities? If so, please describe when and under what circumstances. Why did you do so?

Yes. Before I was marned I lied about using magazines. After I lied when the web sites popped up when my wife was using the computer

_____

_____

_____

_____

Have you downplayed your involvement or failed to be honest about your involvement with cybersex to a spouse, partner, boss, or therapist? If so, when and under what circumstances? Why did you do so?

Yes, Throughout the relationship, Whenever I was asked about porn - I would deny that I used it I would also say that I was against it.

_____

_____

_____

_____

_____

Have you used the "just curious" excuse? If so, when and why?

No

_____

_____

_____

8. Committing Illegal Sexual Acts Online (for Example, Sending or Downloading Child Pornography or Soliciting Illegal Sex Acts Online)

Certain activities on the Internet have been declared illegal in many, if not all, states. As people use the Internet for sex-related activities, and as they increase their time on the Net, some also move closer to engaging in illegal behaviors. A forty-year-old male who'd fantasized about having sex with a teenager for several years eventually began visiting a teen chat room. He engaged in a conversation with a thirteen-year-old female for some time before moving the relationship to a point where he asked where he could meet her to have sex. Soliciting sex acts with minors online is illegal, just as sending, exchanging, or downloading child pornography is illegal. These are felony offenses that, in many states, will result in mandatory prison time.

Are you thinking about such an action? If so, what has stopped you thus far?

No

Have you engaged in an illegal online activity?

No

9. Jeopardizing or Losing a Significant Relationship, Job, or Educational or Career Opportunity Because of Online Sexual Behavior

Online sex-related activities can have serious consequences. Cybersex affairs have ruined marriages. Accessing cybersex sites while at work can result in job termination. Professional and personal reputations have been compromised or ruined. Are parts of your life being affected by your online sexual behavior? If so, please describe in detail.

> Yes. My wife was (and is) very upset about
> me going online and master bating

Have you jeopardized or lost a significant relationship due to cybersex use? If so, please describe.

Have you lost a job, jeopardized your career or college education, or risked your health and well-being because of cybersex activities? If so, please describe.

> no

10. Incurring Significant Financial Consequences as a Result of Engaging in Online Sexual Behavior

While basic Internet access can be fairly inexpensive, many cybersex sites charge a monthly access fee. A thirty-two-year-old male client was shocked when he opened his credit card bill one day to find charges totaling more than $1,200. He'd been registering to enter various cybersex sites and had completely lost track of how many he'd paid for. A twenty-three-year-old female client received an Internet server bill for hundreds of dollars. She'd spent six or so hours per day in chat rooms and had sailed miles past her "free minutes" limit without realizing that charges were accruing. Another male client spent $40,000 in one month dating high-priced call girls and using cocaine. He'd arranged for both through an online prostitution service.

How many cybersex site memberships are you paying for each month? __1__

What are your monthly Internet fees? __19.99__

Have you felt the financial consequences of your time online? If so, please describe.

__no__

Have you lost job or educational opportunities because of your time online? If so, describe.

__no__

What It Means for You

We assume that you are reading this workbook because you or others who care about you are concerned about your use of the Internet for sex-related activities. The most important step you can take now is to look honestly at your Internet behavior and at the consequences of that behavior. Perhaps you're spending more time than you really want in sex-related Internet activities. This should sound an alarm indicating that something is out of balance and that you need to take action and seek help.

As you read through the ten criteria for problematic cybersex behavior described above, which ones most applied to your life?

Number Nine ~ risking a significant relationship

_____

_____

_____

_____

If three or more of these ten criteria for problematic sexual behavior apply to you, your online activities are probably causing difficulties in your life, and the sooner you act to make changes, the easier it will be for you to overcome this problem.

Exercise 3: Internet Sex Screening Test

Completing the following Internet Sex Screening Test will help you further examine your online behavior.

Read each statement carefully and answer honestly. If the statement is true or mostly true for you, mark the blank with a T. If it is false or mostly false, mark the blank with an F.

F 1. I have some sexual sites bookmarked.

F 2. I spend more than five hours per week using my computer for sexual pursuits.

T 3. I have joined sexual sites to gain access to online sexual material.

F 4. I have purchased sexual products online.

T 5. I have searched for sexual material through an Internet search tool.

F 6. I have spent more money for online sexual material than I planned.

F 7. Internet sex has sometimes interfered with certain aspects of my life.

T 8. I have participated in sexually related chats.

F 9. I have a sexualized user name or nickname that I use on the Internet.

T 10. I have masturbated while on the Internet.

F 11. I have accessed sexual sites from other computers besides my own.

T 12. No one knows I use my computer for sexual purposes.

F 13. I have tried to hide what is on my computer or monitor so others cannot see it.

T 14. I have stayed up after midnight to access sexual material online.

F 15. I use the Internet to experiment with different aspects of sexuality such as bondage, and anal sex.

F 16. I have my own Web site that contains sexually explicit material.

T 17. I have made promises to myself to stop using the Internet for sexual purposes.

T 18. I sometimes use cybersex as a reward for accomplishing something like finishing a project or enduring a stressful day.

F 19. When I am unable to access sexual information online, I feel anxious, angry, or disappointed.

F 20. I have increased the risks I take online (for example, giving out my real name and phone number or meeting people offline).

F 21. I have punished myself for using the Internet for sexual purposes. For example, I've arranged time-out from the computer or canceled Internet subscriptions.

T 22. I have met face-to-face with someone I met online for romantic purposes.

F 23. I use sexual humor and innuendo with others while online.

F 24. I have run across illegal sexual material while on the Internet.

F 25. I believe I am an Internet sex addict.

Total number of statements marked "true": _7_

Total number of statements marked "false": _13_

Scoring the Internet Sex Screening Test[2]

Give yourself one point for each statement that you marked "true." Based on 935 people who have previously taken this test, we have found that if your score is 19 or above, it is very likely that you have a problem with your online sex-related activities.

You've taken an important, positive first step by reading this workbook and showing a willingness to begin addressing this problem. Be assured that you can find help here to better understand and regain control over your online sex-related behavior.

On the other hand, you may not recognize that you have a problem. If you see a pattern in your Internet behavior that seems similar to the problematic behavior we've explored thus far, this may be an indication that you are at risk. In that case, you would do well to learn more about your behavior and about your reasons for using the Internet for sexual activities. If you can relate to only some examples, or if you believe that your partner might have a problem with online sexual behavior, we urge you to still continue this workbook.

Remember that no set of criteria or test is an absolutely accurate measure or indication of a problem. Screening tests like this one are based on the behavior of many people; they are not capable of measuring individual differences or of addressing every kind of behavior. Scoring between 9 and 19 could indicate that you have some behaviors that may be problematic or that will eventually become problematic.

If you don't feel you have a problem with cybersex and you scored below 19 on the screening, but you are reading this workbook at the suggestion of someone who cares about you, pay attention. It's important to continue. Those who know us well can often see our lives and our behaviors in ways we cannot. It's difficult to be objective with ourselves. It's important to realize that others may see something that you don't recognize.

We also want to remind you that problematic cybersex behaviors lie on a continuum ranging from those that are relatively harmless to those that are compulsive or addictive and that pose serious health, relationship, and legal risks.

In chapter 3, we will begin to give you the tools you need to deal effectively with your problematic cybersex behaviors. You'll learn more about the process of making permanent change in your life. And you'll learn about three kinds of change: first order, transitional, and second order.

CHAPTER 3: *Preparing for Change*

Making changes in our lives can be difficult. Each year in late January or early February, for example, we hear stories from friends about New Year's resolutions that have fallen by the wayside. Descriptions of failed diets, smoking cessation programs, or exercise plans are ubiquitous. You, too, have likely made promises to yourself about changing your cybersex behavior, only to find you've been unable to keep them.

Making life changes happen takes more than a promise to yourself. While it is often difficult, the success of countless people who have done so is proof that it's possible. That's what this and the next two chapters are about: learning how to make and maintain the changes you've decided are best for you.

First, we'd like to help you look more closely at the process of change. In their book *Changing for Good*, authors James Prochaska, John Norcross, and Carlos DiClemente state that there are six steps, or stages, that people go through when making changes in their lives, regardless of their goal.[1] For example, if you think about a specific problem that you have resolved, chances are you will recognize immediately that its resolution didn't happen all at once. Perhaps for a while you ignored the problem; then you considered tackling it; after that, you may have made definite plans to change. Then, once you had garnered your forces—mental, physical, and social—you acted and began to struggle with the problem. If you succeeded, you worked at maintaining this change. If you failed, you probably gave up for a time, went back to the drawing board, and then tried once more.

Each of these steps is a predictable, well-defined stage: it takes place over a period of time and includes a series of tasks that must be completed before moving on to the next stage. Each stage doesn't inevitably lead to the next; it is possible to become stuck at one stage or another. However, by understanding these stages, you can gain control over the cycle of change and move through it more quickly and efficiently—and with less struggle.

As you read through these stages, we suggest that you keep in mind some changes that you've made, or tried to make, in your life and try to see how these stages apply to them. At the end of this section, we'll ask you to describe a change you've made, or tried to make, and relate the process you used to the process we're about to describe.

Stage 1: Precontemplation

In this stage, it's not that you can't see the solution; it's that you can't see the problem! People at this stage usually have no intention of changing their behavior and typically deny having a problem. Although family members, friends, neighbors, doctors, or co-workers can see the problem quite clearly, the typical person in this stage can't.

Most people in this stage don't want to change themselves, just the people around them. Often, they come to therapy because of pressure from others—a partner who threatens to leave them, an employer who threatens to fire them, or judges who threaten to punish them. Their first response in therapy is often, "How can I get others to quit nagging me?" When all else fails, they may change, but only as long as there is constant outside pressure. When that's gone, they quickly return to their old ways.

Precontemplators resist change. When their problem comes up in conversation, they shift the subject. They lack information about it and they intend to maintain ignorant bliss at all costs. Denial is characteristic of precontemplators, who place the responsibility for their problems on factors such as genetic makeup, family, society, or whatever, all of which they see as being out of their control. Precontemplators also tend to be demoralized as well. They don't want to think, talk, or read about their problems because they feel the situation is hopeless.

So how can you change if you don't want to? The answer is in the approach; even precontemplators will progress toward change if they have the proper tools at the proper time.

Stage 2: Contemplation

"I want to stop feeling stuck." These words are typical of contemplators. In the contemplation stage, people acknowledge that they have a problem and begin to think seriously about solving it. Contemplators struggle to understand their problem, to see its causes, and to wonder about possible solutions. Many have indefinite plans to take action within the next six months or so.

In this stage, you have become aware that something is amiss in your life. You've begun noticing that some "difficulties" have arisen. Your work supervisor recently had a meeting with you specifically to talk about those missed deadlines and the fact that you've been late getting to work more and more often. You know that both situations are due to your increasing cybersex involvement. The thought occurs to you that perhaps cybersex is a "bit of a problem." You contemplate making some changes, putting some controls on your use, and cutting down a bit.

The nature of contemplation can seem puzzling: you know your destination and even how to get there, but you are not quite ready to go yet. Many people remain in this stage for a long time. Many spend years telling themselves that someday, they'll change. When contemplators begin the transition to the preparation stage, their thinking is clearly marked by two changes. First, they begin to focus on the solution rather than the problem. Then they begin to think more about the future than the past. The end of the contemplation stage is a time of anticipation, activity, anxiety, and excitement.

Stage 3: Preparation

Most people in the preparation stage are planning to take action soon, often within the very next month, and are making the final adjustments before they begin to change their behavior. An important step now is to make public the intended change. But although people in this stage are committed to acting and may appear ready to do so, they have not necessarily resolved their ambivalence. They may still need to convince themselves that this is what is best for them. People in the preparation stage may already have instituted a number of small behavioral changes, such as cutting their cigarette intake or counting calories. Awareness is high, and anticipation is palpable. People who cut short this stage—for example, waking up one morning and deciding to quit smoking cold turkey—actually lower their chances of success. It's better to make use of this time by planning carefully, developing a firm, detailed scheme for action, and making sure that you have learned the change processes you need to carry you through the process.

You might be asking yourself questions like, "Do I need to get rid of the computer altogether?" "Do I need to put limits on how much time I spend on the computer or where I use it?" "What do I need to be cautious of?" "What is it exactly that I need to change?" In other words, what preparations do you need to make to effect the change?

Often anxiety is the impetus for finally taking action. While anxiety is often seen as a negative state, in this case, it has a positive effect in that it can impel us to finally move out of contemplation and into preparation and action. Without anxiety, there is often no change. If life is comfortable, why rock the boat? Concern and discomfort push us to take action to relieve anxiety.

Stage 4: Taking Action

The action stage is the one in which people most obviously change their behavior and their surroundings. They stop smoking cigarettes, remove all tempting desserts from the house, pour the last beer down the drain, send all the pornography to the dump, or confront their fears. In short, they make the move they've been planning.

The danger in this stage is that many people, including professional therapists, often mistakenly equate action with change, overlooking not only the critical work that prepares people for successful action but the equally important (and often more challenging) efforts to maintain the changes following action.

It's important to recognize that the action stage is not the only time you can make progress toward overcoming your problem. Although modifying your behavior is the most visible form of change, it is far from the only one: you can also change your level of awareness, emotions, self-image, thinking, and so on. And many of those changes take place in the stages that precede action.

Furthermore, any movement from one stage of change to the next represents considerable progress. If, after years of avoiding a problem, you consciously begin to acknowledge that it exists and think seriously about changing it, the transition from precontemplation to contemplation is no less significant than from preparation to action.

Stage 5: Maintenance

There are great challenges at every stage, and the maintenance stage is no exception. It is here that people must work to consolidate the gains that they have made during the previous stages and struggle to prevent lapses and relapse. Change never ends with action. Although traditional therapy sees maintenance as a static stage, in fact it is a critically important continuation that can last from as little as six months to the rest of one's life. Without a strong commitment to maintenance, there will surely be relapse, usually to the precontemplation or contemplation stages. Programs that promise easy change—crash diets, one-day smoking cessation sessions, or whatever—usually fail to acknowledge that maintenance is a long, ongoing process.

Stage 6: Relapse

While Prochaska and his colleagues described this change process in a linear sequence—precontemplation, contemplation, preparation, action, maintenance—life is not so clear-cut and simple. Most people do slip up at some point, returning to earlier stages before renewing their efforts.

Relapse means slipping back into the behaviors you've decided to leave behind. Prochaska and many others who help people make changes in their lives strongly emphasize several points about relapse. First, relapse is a normal part of the change process. Making changes is not like flipping a light switch—as in, "I did things this way yesterday," and now (flipping the switch) "I'll do those things differently today." The average successful self-changer relapses several times.

Needless to say, the feelings relapse evokes are not pleasant. You may feel like a complete failure, embarrassed, ashamed, and guilty and may believe that all of your hard efforts at change have been wasted. Demoralization sets in, and you may want to give up on changing entirely. You may slide all the way back to the precontemplation stage.

After several setbacks, you may feel as though you are going in circles. But you're not. Think of the change cycle not as a circle, but as an upward spiral. You may be in the contemplation or planning stage again, but this time you can draw on the lessons you've learned from your previous efforts. Relapse, or recycling, gives you the opportunity to learn. Viewed in this way, relapsing into old behaviors is not a failure, but rather a learning experience. You've prepared and taken action. Then, when you slip up, you simply move back to stages 2 and 3 to reevaluate what you're doing, how you slipped, and what you can do to minimize the chances of future relapse. Your goal is to learn from your slip. Prochaska says we can always expect some level of relapse to occur, particularly if the change is a difficult one such as dealing with cybersex. Taking action and slipping is much better than taking no action at all.

Choose one change you've tried to make. It might be one you made successfully

Exercise 1: Describing a Change You've Attempted

or one that you weren't able to completely accomplish—quitting smoking, losing weight, starting an exercise program, taking up a new hobby, spending more time with your child, being more organized at work, cleaning the house on a regular schedule, or staying in closer touch with a friend, for example. Describe the process you went through, beginning with the very moment you began thinking about making this change.

LOOSING WEIGHT

WANTED TO LOOSE WEIGHT TO BE
HEALTHIER, REDUCE STRAIN ON BACK, BE MORE
ACTIVE

COMMITED TO LOOSING AS MUCH WIEGHT
AS A CONTEST IN APRIL, AND WAS PAIRED
WITH A PARTNER TO SUPPORT ME

Next, refer to the six stages of change we've just described. In the spaces below, jot down the steps you went through in each stage.

Stage 1: Precontemplation

RESISTED I NEEDED TO LOOSE WIEGHT

THOUGHT I WASNT THAT OVERWRIGHT

HAD OTHER THINGS TO WORRY ABOUT

EATING MADE ME FEEL GOOD

Stage 2: Contemplation

HEARD FROM DOCTOR THAT I NEEDED TO

LOOSE WIEGHT

GOT DMV PICTURE

Stage 3: Preparation

GOT VITAMINS / SHAKES

SET TIME PERIOD

Stage 4: Taking Action

STARTED PLAN

WIEGHED IN

Stage 5: Maintenance

TOOK VITAMINS

CONTINUED TO WIEGH IN .

Stage 6: Relapse

DAYS WHERE I DONT HAVE TIME
TO EAT 'RIGHT' GOT MORE AND MORE

How far did you progress in terms of the six stages?

ALL SIX

Did you get stuck? If so, at what stage (or stages)?

STAGE SIX, RAN OUT OF DIET VITAMINS / SUPPLEMENTS

Did you have to go back to a previous stage? If so, to which one?

STAGE 5, STARTED DOING PLAN W/O PARTNER

How did you feel when you got stuck?

SAD, HOPELESS

Do you think you would have felt differently about this if you'd known more about the process of change? Or, given what you now know about the process, do you view what happened differently now? Please explain.

WOULD DO MORE PREPEZATION
MORE (BETTER) SUPPORTS

You may find that you will cycle through these stages in various areas of your life at different levels for many years. Let's say, for example, that you've come to grips with your cybersex behavior. It's no longer a problem. Then, however, you notice that the relationship between you and your partner isn't all that you want it to be . . . so you apply the change process to this issue.

In its broadest sense, this change and recovery process is really a way of living life more fully and consciously. It's not something that you do for a few days, weeks, or months and then say, "Great! That's done. Time to move on."

Remember that while we are applying these stages to the problem of cybersex, everyone moves through them when they make any change in their life. The stages are applicable to all behaviors, whether relatively harmless of seriously dysfunctional.

Making Changes

Before we look at specific changes you can make in your cybersex behavior, we want to introduce you to three levels of change—First Order, Transition, and Second Order changes.[2] First Order changes are very concrete actions that are taken to quickly stop a problem and to address specific consequences. First Order changes are also well-described by the French aphorism "The more things change, the more they remain the same." For example, think of Marie, a woman who'd been married three times, each time to an alcoholic. She changed husbands, but still found herself in the same situation. She did not change her life with each marriage. Instead, she continued to marry and live with alcoholics. First Order change won't help anyone solve a compulsive or addictive behavior on a permanent basis.

It is important to understand that compulsion or addiction of any kind is a First Order phenomenon. The harder people struggling with these behaviors try to stop their behavior alone and in secret, the more their failure is guaranteed. Only when they seek help for their problem will they be able to begin making the Second Order changes needed to free themselves of these behaviors.

Second Order changes are those steps that you take to actually change the dynamics of your life and the way you live. Second Order changes for Marie, for example, would include going to therapy and temporarily stopping dating. During therapy, she learns that the lessons she internalized growing up in an alcoholic family form the basis for her selection of men.

To further illustrate the difference between these two types of change, imagine that you have just been injured in an auto accident. When the paramedics arrive, the first action they take is to determine if you're breathing. Then they look for and control any severe bleeding that could bring immediate death. They would also immobilize any broken bones at this time. First Order changes are the splints, airways, and pressure bandages needed to take care of the obvious and immediate problems. They will stabilize your life in the short run. However, if you have internal injuries, your life will still be in danger. Treating only the superficial wounds won't save your life. Dealing with such injuries takes more time and care, as well as professional help. You therefore need Second Order changes to heal and completely recover from more serious problems. Second Order changes take more time, but eventually the whole person is healed, inside and out.

You may be tempted to skip over the First Order changes and go straight to the Second Order changes. Carrying our analogy further illustrates why this is a bad idea. Focusing only on the internal injuries—with "Second Order" care—would not be effective because you'd die of hemorrhage or shock before treatment for the internal injuries could begin. Thus, both first- and Second Order changes play a crucial role in healing.

Transition changes serve as the bridge between First and Second order changes and contain elements of both types. We will look more closely at Transition changes in chapter 5

Exercise 2: First Order, Transition, and Second Order Changes

The following exercise will help you better understand the concepts of First Order, Transition, and Second Order changes. Don't worry if the differences still seem a bit unclear. The information and exercises in chapters four, five, and six will make them clear. Right now, we simply want you to have a general idea of these concepts in preparation for the work in the coming chapters.

The **behaviors** listed below are ones typically taken by a person who is attempting to lose weight. In the space next to each behavior, mark whether you think it is a First Order, Transition, or Second Order change. Our answers are upside down at the bottom of the page. **F** = First Order, **T** = Transition, and **S** = Second Order.

1. _____ S _____ Joining a support group.

2. _____ F _____ Buying healthier groceries, such as fruits and vegetables.

3. _____ S _____ Planning weekly menus that are enticing, yet nutritious, low in fat, and include some favorite foods.

4. _____ S _____ Attending an overeaters support group regularly.

5. _____ S _____ Looking at how stress influences your eating.

6. _____ S _____ Looking at the feelings you have when you want to overeat.

7. _____ S _____ Planning what to do in case of a relapse.

8. _____ F _____ Buying some clothes in a smaller size than currently fits as an incentive.

9. _____ F _____ Researching various weight-loss programs to see which ones work.

10. _____ F _____ Getting rid of all candy and other sweets in the house, as well as fattening junk foods like chips.

11. _____ S _____ Determining what things in your life seem to impel you to eat too much.

12. _____ S _____ Keeping a personal daily journal or diary.

13. _____ F _____ Counting calories.

14. _____ F _____ Starting an exercise routine.

15. _____ F _____ Choosing healthy restaurants.

16. _____ S _____ Keeping a food diary.

In Conclusion

In this chapter, you've looked at the process of change. You've learned more about how you have moved through this process at other times in your life. We have also introduced you to three kinds of change: First Order, Transition, and Second Order.

All of your work in this and the previous chapters has been important and necessary to set the stage for actually addressing and effectively dealing with your problem with cybersex behaviors. In the next chapter, we will help you take the first steps needed to get control of your cybersex behaviors. The final chapters of the book will help you make these changes permanent.

CHAPTER 4: *Making First Order Changes*

As you begin this chapter, we ask you to bring to the front of your mind just what it is about cybersex that has been so appealing to you. You might look back at the work you did in chapter one (exercise 1) in which we asked you to look at the six CyberHex characteristics—Intoxicating, Isolating, Integral, Imposing, Interactive, and Inexpensive—and what influence they have on you. Which were most appealing? How did each of them pull you into the Net and cybersex? Before you can take steps to change your cybersex behavior, it's important to be aware of exactly what is appealing about it. The exercises that follow focus on each of the six CyberHex characteristics.

It is likely that some crisis related to your cybersex activities has prompted you to seek help for this problem. Maybe your boss caught you surfing porn sites while on the job. Perhaps your spouse or partner discovered your cybersex bookmarks on your computer. Perhaps you've just had a negative online experience or a bad offline experience related to your cybersex activities, or perhaps you feel great shame about what you've been doing. Whatever the reason, something has brought you to the point of saying, "I've got to stop this." You've realized that you simply have to take some action to get these behaviors under control.

This is a very common experience. Crises tend to force us to make changes in our lives. The information and exercises in this chapter are designed to help you put an immediate stop to your cybersex activities. This is a "damage control" mode, so to speak. Once you've gotten some control over these behaviors, you will be able to get the additional help you need to look more closely at your life and see what factors have played a role in your out-of-control cybersex behavior. You'll then be able to take steps to defuse these triggers and to live a richer and more meaningful life without cybersex.

Exercise 1: Summarizing Your Problematic Cybersex Usage

The first step in controlling your cybersex behavior is to develop a crisis management plan. But before you can do this, you have to be clear about what you have to manage. To do this, we ask you to refer to exercise 1 in chapter 2 where you developed an Internet activity log. Review your use of the Internet and answer the following questions:

What days of the week do you use the Net for cybersex?

AND DAY (NOT SPECIFIC)

How many hours a day are you using the Net for cybersex?

1/2 TO AN HOUR, MAY AVERAGE 10-20 MINUTES

What times of day do you use the Net for cybersex?

LATE NIGHT

Where do you use the Net for cybersex?

TO MASTERBATE WHICH
· RELIEVED STRESS AND SEXAUL TENSION
· RELAXATION

DOWNSTAIRS AT COMPUTER

Why do you use the Net for cybersex?

What are you feeling when you use the Net for cybersex?

FRUSTRATED
· BORED
LONELY
HORNY

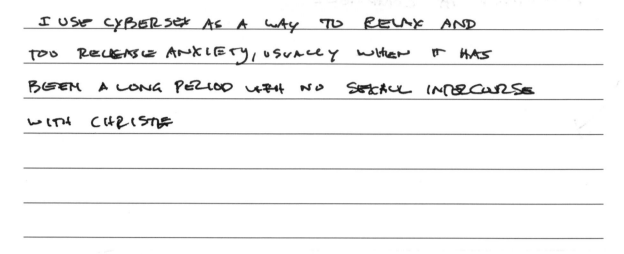

This exercise gives you a clear summary of where, when, and why you use the Net for cybersex. Perhaps you see that you get into trouble if you spend more than two hours online. Part of your crisis management plan might then be to limit yourself to forty-five minutes a day online, just enough to answer e-mail and take care of your business. Or, you may see that youhave problems with cybersex only at work or only at home. Looking at your patterns will help you create your crisis management plan.

What patterns do you see in your cybersex behavior?

I USE CYBERSEX AS A WAY TO RELAX AND
TOO RELEASE ANXIETY, USUALLY WHEN IT HAS
BEEN A LONG PERIOD WITH NO SEXUAL INTERCOURSE
WITH CHRISTIE

Keep these patterns in mind as you read through the following suggestions for making First Order changes to halt your cybersex behaviors.

Examples of First Order Changes

The boundaries of First Order change may seem very restrictive. That's because, for now, you need clear and strong external limits and controls. Then, as you gain more control over your behaviors and your life, you'll be able to modify or lessen these restrictions.

The First Order changes you need to put into effect fit into five categories—reducing access, reducing anonymity, reducing objectification, making yourself accountable, and beginning to develop healthy online habits.

First and foremost, you cannot make these changes in your life alone. We have seen many, many people try to do so, only to fail. Having a good sponsor in your life is perhaps the most important part of your own commitment to make changes in your life. Your sponsor will be the person you can turn to in a crisis, the one you can call at 2:00 a.m., the person who can give you a kick in the pants when you are procrastinating and who can give you hope when you are thinking that life just won't get better. We have found that having a good sponsor can make all the difference in beginning and maintaining a successful recovery. Without a good sponsor, you reduce your chances of success despite your best intentions and hard work. Remember, you can't do this alone! And if you think about that for a moment, you'll probably realize that you've proven that statement's accuracy to yourself many times.

Choosing a sponsor is a very important decision. Because you will tell this person the details of your cybersex activities along with a good deal of other information about your sexuality and personal life, your sponsor must be a person in whom you have—or can develop—a high level of trust. This person must also take your behaviors seriously and not minimize your chances for relapsing. Your sponsor must be someone you respect and to whom you'll listen even when you're being told something you don't want to hear.

Take care when choosing your sponsor. You may be inclined to turn to your spouse or partner. He or she may not, however, be the best choice for this task. Spouses and partners are too close to the problem and consequently are often too emotionally invested in you and your relationship to be objective enough for this role. At some point, it will very likely be important to tell your spouse about your cybersex involvement and that will be one of your goals.

Here are some questions to ask yourself that will help you choose someone to whom you can tell your story.

- Can this person be objective and supportive?
- Can I trust this person with this information?
- Can this person be nonjudgmental?
- Will this information hurt this person? (It's important that the person you tell will not be hurt by knowing your story.)
- Can this person serve as a resource in helping me find others to tell, or for finding additional help for my problem?

If you cannot identify anyone to serve in this role, you must develop a plan to bring such a person into your life. Begin by looking closely at all the people in your life, even those you don't know very well. Sometimes it is possible to develop a stronger relationship with one of them—and cultivating a sponsor relationship from this group is usually easier than starting from scratch.

Exercise 2: Choosing a Sponsor

Step 1: Create a list of the people in your life who could be a potential sponsor; that includes even those who are only remote candidates (adult, persons for whom you have at least some respect). For each person, make a list of reasons why he or she would be a good sponsor and reasons against that choice. Consider the attributes or qualities this person has, such as being truthful, frank, trustworthy, empathetic, able to hold confidences. Disqualifying reasons might include being too busy to take time for you or doesn't believe that cybersex is really a problem.

Rank the people on your list from the best to least acceptable choice.
Choose the top five and talk with your support group about each of them.

PERSON	REASONS FOR	REASONS AGAINST
1. SEAN	HAD A GOOD CONNECTION BEEN THROUGH THE PROCESS	MIGHT NOT BE READY HAVEN'T TALKED TO HIM IN A LONG TIME
2. BRUCE	SMART, LEVEL HEADED SUPPORTIVE	NOT MUCH EXPERIENCE STRUGGLING WITH OWN ISSUES
3. DAN	CLOSEST MALE FRIEND. EASY TO TALK TO.	MAY NOT AGREE THAT SA IS A PROBLEM

PERSON	REASONS FOR	REASONS AGAINST
4. RAY	BEEN IN THERAPY SUPPORTIVE. GOD LISTNER	GOING THROUGH A SEPERATION NOT ANY TIME
5.		

Ask your support group or your therapist which person, if any, would be a good sponsor for you.

Step 2: If you find a potential sponsor through the process in Step 1, then develop a specific plan (including a timetable) with your therapist about how you will develop your sponsor relationship with this person.

It is possible that you will feel as if you do not have anyone in your life you can tell your story to. One of the consequences of compulsive and addictive cybersex use is that you become isolated. You slowly cut yourself off from family and friends. If you don't know anyone with whom you feel safe telling your story, this is another indication that you have made a very wise decision to seek help for your cybersex behaviors.

If this is the case, we strongly urge you to speak to a therapist who has expertise in this area (if you are not already seeing a therapist). If you don't know of a good therapist, you can contact the National Council on Sexual Addiction and Compulsivity, which keeps a reference file of therapists throughout the country who are skilled and experienced in working with people who are dealing with sexually compulsive and addictive behaviors. Please refer to the appendix for more information on this organization and on other resources available to you. Also, see the section in chapter 5 entitled "Finding and Working with a Good Therapist."

Regardless of whether you choose a trusted friend or a therapist to hear you story, you must tell this person *everything*. If you edit, omit, or filter information, you will limit how effective help and therapy can be. The key to success in both therapy and recovery is sharing everything—even your very worst secrets. It's fine to allow yourself to be seen as a "mess"—to admit how out of control you have been. Therapists are trained to help people in these situations. Few decisions are more counterproductive than to reveal critical information in therapy after it's too late. A good therapist will, in fact, ask you whether you've told everything. You need to make a full disclosure. Numerous studies by Dr. Patrick Carnes, the foremost authority on sexual addiction and compulsivity, have shown that sex addicts who made full disclosure did better in recovery than those who did not.

After you disclose your story to one person, you may feel so unburdened and elated that you may want to tell more people. At this point, we ask you to resist this urge. Right now, telling one or, at most, two individuals who can help you set up a plan for dealing with this problem is enough. Later, you will make disclosures to other people when the appropriate time comes, but at this point, don't over-disclose. Be conservative.

Reduce Access

- If your computer is in a relatively private setting in your home, move it into a higher-traffic area that is more regularly frequented by family members. Don't, for example, keep it in a home office, in your bedroom, or in an area where you can close a door for privacy. Instead, move it into your family room.
- Don't go online except when others are at home.
- Set limits for when and how long you can use your computer. In addition, set a curfew for evening use, such as an 11:00 p.m. deadline.
- Use electronic limits to reduce your access on your home computer. Install password protection on your computer—only your spouse, not you, should know the password that will allow you to use the computer.
- Switch to a "safe" Internet service provider. A number of family-oriented Internet service providers, for example, carefully screen out sexual sites and often provide better protection than software like Net Nanny. To find one in your area, type "family-oriented service providers" into a computer search engine such as Google or Yahoo.
- If you were using your computer at work for cybersex, leave your office door open whenever you're using the computer and place your monitor so that others can see it as they walk by.

Reduce Anonymity

- Be sure that your e-mail addresses and screen names actually identify you, even if it's only your real first name. No more hiding behind fictitious identities.
- As we discussed earlier in this chapter, confide in one trusted person about your problem. (Soon we will talk more about disclosing your problem to a few other people who are important in your life.)

Reduce Objectification

- Regularly remind yourself that those with whom you communicate on the Net are real human beings with feelings, hopes, worries, and loved ones and that they can be affected by your interactions with them. The Internet is *not* a video game.

Make Yourself Accountable

- Allow a trusted friend or therapist to monitor your Internet behavior and access. Give this person access to your computer history files. Make yourself accountable to this person for the time you spend online and what you did online.

Develop Healthy Online Habits

It is very important to understand that we are not saying you can't use your computer or the Internet. While that might actually be a good option, the Internet has become such an integral part of our personal and work lives that we just can't avoid using it. You can, however, learn to use the Internet only for healthy purposes by developing healthy online habits and by accessing supportive recovery online resources. For example, you can do the folllowing:

- Get an online sponsor.
- Develop e-mail buddies who are also recovering from problematic online sexual behavior.
- Find and use Web sites that support your recovery rather than undermine it.
- Find and visit online support groups. For example, *One Day at a Time* mailing lists will e-mail you an encouraging and supportive thought each day.

Finding Others to Support Your Recovery Efforts

As you have discovered, people who are involved in cybersex can't be objective enough to decide what they can and can't handle online. For this reason, it's important to seek therapy, join a Twelve Step group or other support group that focuses on this problem, or both. It is also important to find a sponsor, that trusted person with whom you can talk about cybersex and recovery.

While we will talk more about these suggestions in the coming chapters, we feel it's important for you to know that you will need more help—and that help is readily available to you. As you move ahead, try not to be too discouraged. Many people have overcome problematic cybersex behaviors by doing the work we outline in this workbook.

Finding and regularly seeing a therapist can help you in many ways. Often, problems with online sexual behaviors are symptoms of deeper, longer-term problems such as depression or issues growing out of your childhood. Dealing with depression or anxiety requires help from a professional. Some people also find that medications help them with these problems. For all these reasons, we strongly recommend that you get a comprehensive evaluation by a psychiatrist.

You may question whether you really need so much help in dealing with these behaviors. It's important to again acknowledge that you have a problem and that if you'd been able to handle it on your own, you wouldn't be in the spot you're in right now and reading this workbook for help.

Depression and anxiety, for example, have nothing to do with willpower or how strong a person you are. They often have roots in brain chemistry, and for that, you need more help to work through these problems.

We also want to stress the importance of combined therapies. Too often, people seeking help for compulsive or addictive online sexual behavior will select only one source of help, such as a Twelve Step group, group therapy, or seeing a therapist. This strategy can work successfully, but using a combination of therapies increases the likelihood of your success. A comprehensive treatment approach is best. We believe that using individual and group therapy along with recovery groups and medication, if appropriate, is the most effective recovery strategy.

Phase Two of Developing Your Crisis Management Plan

To further develop your crisis management plan, choose one cybersex behavior you need to stop. Then, choose three First Order changes that will help you accomplish this goal. The first (first tier change) should be the least restrictive and least intrusive needed for you to accomplish your goal. Next, add a second, more restrictive and intrusive change (second tier change). Finally, add a third change—the most restrictive and intrusive of the three (third tier change).

There is a good reason for choosing three changes, each progressively more controlling than the previous one. If, after a time, your first tier change is no longer working, you can move to the second tier—and to the third tier, if need be.

Figure 4.1

Tiers of Intervention

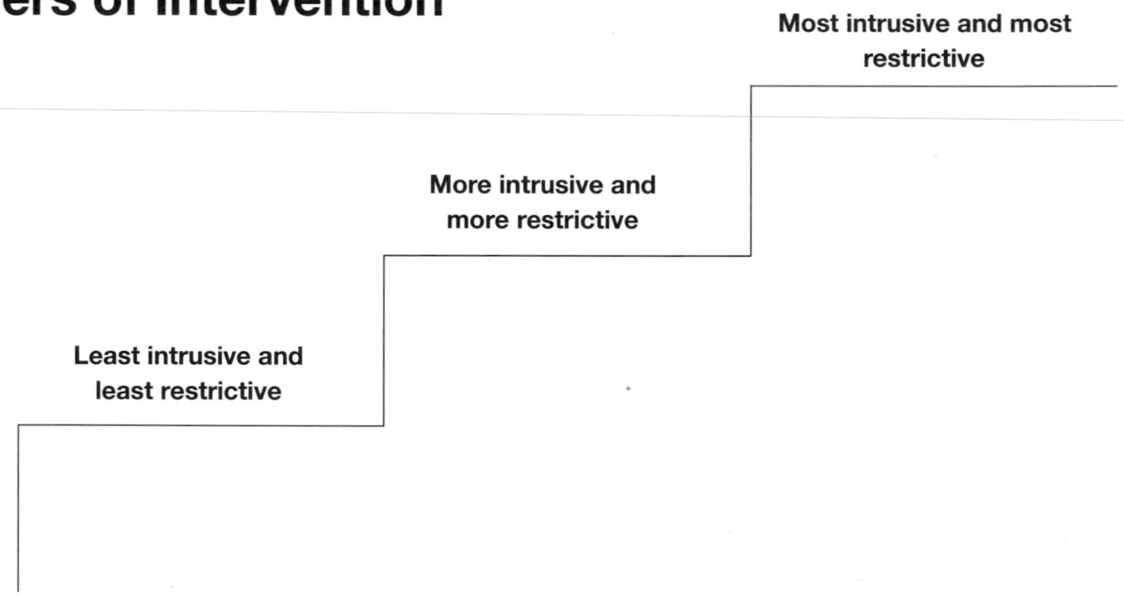

Most intrusive and most restrictive

More intrusive and more restrictive

Least intrusive and least restrictive

Here are two examples to help you better understand what you need to do:

SAMPLE CRISIS MANAGEMENT PLAN #1

Behavior I want to stop:
Using my home computer for cybersex

Third tier change:
I will install password protection on my computer. My wife, not I, will have the password, and thus control of when I can use the computer.

Second tier change:
I will move my computer into a more public area of the house and will use it only when others are home with me.

First tier change:
Since I always do cybersex after my family has gone to bed, I won't use the computer after 10:30 p.m. and will go to bed with my wife.

SAMPLE CRISIS MANAGEMENT PLAN #2

Behavior I want to stop:
Using my computer at work for cybersex.

Third tier change:
I will explain my problem to my system administrator and ask that they block my access to pornography sites or monitor my Internet use.

Second tier change:
I will place my computer monitor in such a way that anyone walking past my office will easily be able to see what I am doing, and I will not use that computer for any personal use.

First tier change:
I will use my work computer for personal use only during my lunch hour.

Exercise 3: Creating Your Own Crisis Management Plan

Now it is time for you to write your crisis management plans. Write a plan for each behavior you need to stop. Be as specific as possible when writing your first, second, and third tier changes.

CRISIS MANAGEMENT PLAN

Behavior I want to stop:

USING CYBERSEX

Third tier change:

- DO DEEP WORK AROUND CHILD HOOD ISSUES THAT CAUSED DESIRES.
- DO MENS GROUP WORK
- GET AND USE A SPONSOR

Second tier change:

GO TO AN SA SPECIALIST
DO COUPLES WORK

First tier change:

CANCEL SUBSCRIPTION

CRISIS MANAGEMENT PLAN

Behavior I want to stop:

USING CYBER SEX

Third tier change:

CHANGE ADMIN PASSWORD

Second tier change:

INSTALL SOFTWARE THAT LIMITS
WEB SURFING

First tier change:

CANCEL SUBSCRIPTIONS

DONT USE COMPUTER IF I AM AT RISK.

ALLOW CHRISTIE TO REVIEW CHECK BOXS

CRISIS MANAGEMENT PLAN

Behavior I want to stop:

_____

_____

Third tier change:

_____

_____

_____

Second tier change:

_____

_____

_____

First tier change:

_____

_____

_____

CRISIS MANAGEMENT PLAN

Behavior I want to stop:

_____

_____

Third tier change:

_____

_____

_____

Second tier change:

_____

_____

_____

First tier change:

_____

_____

_____

Watch for Warning Signs

This is a difficult time. You are trying to make some very difficult changes in your life. By their nature, First Order changes are not permanent and aren't meant to be. In the following chapters, we will help you make the deeper changes necessary for you to recover from your cybersex problems.

In the meantime, here are some warning signs that you may be about to fall back into cybersex behaviors. When you notice them, it's time to get in touch with your sponsor. Immediately.

Emotional signals include anger, anxiety, loneliness, sadness, feeling sorry for yourself.

Physical signals include tiredness, growing excited about being on the Net, entering a trancelike state, a pounding heart, and heightened anticipation.

Behavioral signals can include lying to your spouse about your activities or lashing out angrily at home or at work.

You might also review the points in the above summary and compare it with your Internet use log, paying particular attention to the reasons you use the Internet for sex and what you are feeling when you do. These feelings, in particular, may trigger a relapse, and being aware of when they begin to surface can give you time to call for help.

Exercise 4: Relapse Prevention Worksheet

This exercise can help you become more aware of your lapse and relapse warning signs. A lapse happens when you are very close to doing a cybersex behavior but stop just short of it. A relapse happens when you actually fall back into an old cybersex behavior. Typing the address of a porn Web site or sexual chat room into your Internet access program but stopping short of hitting the "go" button would be a lapse. Doing this and then hitting the "go" button and actually accessing the site would be a relapse. In the next chapter, we will give you more effective strategies to prevent relapse that will incorporate the work you do in this exercise. At this point, however, we want to help you become more aware of your relapse warning signs.

What would constitute a lapse for you? Give three examples.

1. GOING TO A SEXUALLY EXPLICIT WEBSITE

2. MASTERBATING TO ANY SEXUAL EXPLICIT MATERIAL

3. MASTERBATING (RIGHT NOW FOR ANY REASON) IN THE FUTURE TO MAKE MY SELF FEEL BETTER

1. THINKING I DESERVE IT.
2. TURNING ON THE COMPUTER AND SURFING WHEN I AM THINKING ABOUT MASTERBATING

What would constitute a relapse for you? Give three examples.

1. _____

2. _____

3. _____

What are five emotional signals that show you may be at risk for a relapse?

1. BEING SEXAULLY FRUSTRATED AND THINKING ABOUT MASTELBATING TO RELLEVE IT.

2. GETTING MAD AT CHRISTE AND WANTIN TO GET BACK AT HER BY MASTEZBATING

3. _____

4. _____

5. _____

What are five physical signals that you may be on the verge of slipping back into cybersex behaviors?

1. STAYING UP LATE AT NIGHT ON THE COMPUTER

2. SURFING THE INTERNET FOR NO REASON

3. _____

4. STAYING UP WHEN I AM TIRED

5. NOT BEING ABLE TO SLEEP

What are five behavioral signals that show you may be on the verge of slipping back into cybersex behaviors?

1. _____

2. _____

3. _____

4. _____

5. _____

List five concrete (First Order) steps you could take to avoid lapsing or relapsing.

1. CANCELLING SUBSRIPTNG

2. GOING TO THERAPY

3. ALLOWING CHRISTIE TO REVIEW FINANCIAL RECORDS

4. NOT WEB SURPING SEXALL SITES

5. _____

While this final step may be a bit difficult for you, as you move further through this book, you will be able to develop more effective coping strategies.

① CALL SOMEONE IF YOU FEEL LIKE ACTING OUT.
② GO TO A GROUP MEETING IF I AM IN DANGER OR RELAPSE

Exercise 5: Writing Your Fantasy—to Its Ultimate Conclusion!

You have likely had many fantasies connected with your use of cybersex. These fantasies, however, are only that. They are only what we want them to be. Have you ever thought about what would happen if one of your fantasies would actually happen? What would its real-life conclusion be? Thinking through this scenario is exactly what we are going to ask you to do now.

Begin by choosing one of your cybersex fantasies. In the space below, we want you to write about this fantasy. Describe the place you're in, the person or persons you're with, what's happening—all the details you can imagine. What would you like to have happen? What will happen when it's over? How will it have changed your life?

HAVING SEX WITH TWO WOMEN.

THE WOMEN ARE MODELS (VERY ATRACTIVE)

THEY SAY THEY WANT TO BE SEXUAL WITH ME

WE HAVE SEX FOR MANY TIMES FOR HOURS AND HOURS

Next, we want you to pick up where you ended your cybersex fantasy and carry its completion into the real world.

What would happen if this fantasy actually took place?

ONE OF MY SEXUAL ONLINE FANTASYES WOULD COME TRUE

. I WOULD FEEL MORE CONFIDENT ABOUT ME

What would you get out of this experience?

CONFIDENCE, THE FEELING THAT I AM ATTRACTIVE

Who would be affected by it?

MY WIFE WOULD BE BETRAYED (AGAIN)

I WOULD HAVE DISHONORED MY VOW TO HER

What would happen if your spouse, partner, boss, children, or friends found out about this?

_____

_____

_____

_____

How would they be affected?

SADNESS, ANGER, P.

_____

_____

_____

What would their reactions be?

LEAVE THE RELATIONSHIP/END OF MARRIAGE

_____

_____

_____

Would anyone be hurt? If so, who?

MY WIFE, ME, OUR FAMILIES AND FRIENDS

_____

_____

_____

_____

This exercise can help you see that one result of your cybersex activities is that you've been living in a fantasy world. You have lost touch with reality and with those who care about you. You have been losing touch with reality and the impact of your cybersex behaviors.

Though You're Beginning to Feel Better, Take Care!

Once you begin applying the First Order changes and begin to gain control of your cybersex behaviors, one of the first things you will notice is that you are feeling good—perhaps better than you've felt in a long time.

Once you start to feel better, you may be tempted to stop doing this work. You'll think that you've got the problem under control at last and that there's nothing more to be done. This is akin to taking aspirin for pain. The pain may lessen, but you still need to find out why it was there in the first place.

Here's the typical cycle that people trying to recover from compulsive or addictive cybersex behaviors experience: they feel better, they want to stop working on the problem, they have another crisis, they go back to the process again.

Exercise 6: Past Changes You've Made to Control Cybersex Behaviors

Have you tried to stop your cybersex behaviors before—but failed? Perhaps the steps you took were essentially First Order changes. Take a moment to list some examples of changes that you have made in the past in an effort to control your cybersex behaviors.

1. CANCELLED SUBSCRIPTION TO WEBSITE

2. VOWED I WOULD STOP

3.

4.

5.

What were you hoping to accomplish by attempting these changes?

WANTED TO BE MORE HONEST

WANTED TO MOVE ON

WANTED TO STOP LYING ALL

What were the results of your attempts?

AFTER A WHILE I STARTED SURFING AGAIN WHEN I WAS SEXUALLY FRUSTRATED.

Were the changes you made essentially First Order? _*YES*_

This exercise has probably shown you that First Order changes are only temporarily effective; long-term change requires additional steps. Likewise, while First Order changes will help you control your cybersex behaviors in the short term, you need to do more work to make these changes permanent and to recover from your compulsive behaviors. The information and exercises in chapter 5 will help you begin this process.

It is, however, important for you to know that the good feeling you will experience you make First Order changes is real. It is a glimpse at what life can be when you arefree of compulsive and addictive behaviors. This is what you can achieve. But to do so in the long run, you need to continue working. You may even feel worse again during this process before you feel good again. But don't lose heart. That's just part of the process. You need to finish the work in this workbook.

It's likely, in fact, that you will have setbacks. If so, try not to feel ashamed or to feel that you've failed. Remember the steps to change we spoke about in chapter 3. This is just part of the process of growth and change. Recovery is about taking more steps forward than you do backward. And perhaps most important, remember that you *are* doing something positive. You're trying to change and grow. Give yourself a lot of credit for this. You have taken a big and important step forward.

CHAPTER 5: *Making the Transition to Lifelong Change and Recovery*

We've called this phase of recovery Transition changes because that's exactly the purpose of the steps you're about to take: to help you make the transition from the temporary, stopgap measures of First Order change to the steps of Second Order change that promote long-term recovery.

At this point in this process, people struggling with compulsive or addictive behaviors often see their lives in "black and white" terms. They see themselves as in recovery or not in recovery—as either succeeding or failing in their efforts to deal with their compulsive or addictive behaviors.

One of the most important lessons you can learn now is that recovery is a process, not a state of being. It is a slow and steady process of change, discovery, and personal growth. Remember how the stages of change we examined in chapter 3 were not absolute. They overlapped at times—so you can be in more than one stage at the same time. And you may have to return occasionally to previous stages before moving ahead once again. That's what the recovery process is like, too.

The steps in this Transition phase will help you eventually move toward the Second Order changes that need to happen in your life for long-term recovery to take place. In this phase, you'll discover that you have to do more than just manage the crisis if you want to leave these problematic behaviors behind. The work here will increase your awareness of who you are as a person and what your life has been like. You'll also discover what steps you need to take to make Second Order changes work.

During this Transitional phase, it is common to feel more stress, worry, and strain. The First Order changes helped you manage your crises, but now you will begin to look more closely at yourself to discover the consequences of your out-of-control cybersex behaviors. Some of those good feelings you had after initially getting control of your behaviors will fade away as you see how unmanageable your life has become because of your behaviors. You'll begin to see that your life has to change, that a few First Order changes won't magically make all your problems go away. You'll see that the changes required of you will be more difficult than you expected. Your life will have to change in some fundamental ways. And these realizations will bring pain and grief.

It's not unusual in this Transition stage for feelings of depression and anxiety to increase, and when this happens, people often fall back into their old behaviors. They don't know what to do with these feelings, so they return to old habits and coping mechanisms—cybersex. This reaction can become a vicious cycle: a crisis occurs, causing them to make some First Order changes to control their behavior; they feel better and begin to enter the Transition stage; they start to feel worse again and return to their compulsive or addictive behaviors.

Frank's story illustrates this problem well:

As a forty-something doctor, I had been having problems with cybersex for a couple years, and finally, it was interfering with my medical practice so much that I simply had to do something. I sought help from a therapist and made some changes to control my behavior; specifically, I had password protection put on my computer at work and discontinued my Internet service at home. As I moved out of the crisis stage in recovery, I began to realize that a lot of my problems had to do with my relationship with my wife and how unhappy I was in my marriage—issues I'd never before addressed. I started becoming more and more depressed and angry about all of this. I then found ways to ignore the changes I'd made and fell back into my cybersex behaviors.

Frank repeated this cycle several times before finally breaking free of it to move more firmly into Second Order recovery.

Feeling so much better with your First Order changes in place, you may believe that you are ready to jump right from some First Order change into the deeper work of Second Order change, bypassing this Transition stage altogether. This is another example of black-and-white thinking. If you do this, you will miss out on some of the very important work in this stage.

Denial of the depth of your problem also plays a role at this point. It's not too difficult for people who've been struggling with their cybersex behaviors to acknowledge that they're in a crisis, that their behavior is out of control, and that they have to do something about it. But it's much harder, however, to admit that you have a deeper and ongoing problem. This requires you to move from thinking "this is a problem" to "I have problems"—a much more difficult admission. It's easy to tell yourself that First Order changes will be enough in your situation, or that your problem isn't as bad as most people's, so you only need to do the First Order changes to fix the problem. You might find yourself making such excuses as:

"Now that the crisis is over, I'm feeling a lot better; it mustn't have been that big a problem after all."

"Other people are worse off than I am, so I don't need to do as much as they do."

"I've been doing really well with the First Order things. I don't need to go any further. It's working."

Such attempts at minimization and justification typically come into play during the Transition stage. We'll talk about ways to avoid or overcome such thinking later in this chapter. You might also refer to the exercises you did in chapter 2 to remind yourself of the reality of your problems with cybersex.

Time for a Therapeutic and/or Medical Evaluation?

If you have feelings of anxiety or depression that seem to be worsening, we strongly suggest that you see a psychiatrist who can help you determine whether medications are an appropriate course of action. Your therapist would be a good person to speak with for an appropriate referral to a psychiatrist. Many people find that they cannot stop obsessive or addictive sexual behaviors without the help of medication. This does not mean that they have "failed" in their attempts at recovery. Rather, they have found that the cause of their behaviors lies in a neurochemistry imbalance that no amount of effort or therapy will affect.

Regardless of whether you decide to have a medical evaluation, this is still a good time to begin seeing a therapist on a regular basis to help you work on some of the issues that have contributed to your problematic or addictive cybersex behaviors.

Widening the Circle of People Who Can Help You

The following suggestions will further help you make the transition to effective and meaningful Second Order changes. These steps can enable you to develop a new life in recovery. As you have seen, this is a difficult journey, one that often requires a number of interventions, including therapy, support groups, and spiritual guidance. It also takes time. It may help you to have more patience if you remember that it took you some time to get into the situation you're in, and it will likewise take some time and work for a change to take place.

We stressed earlier in the book how important it is to find a sponsor—a person whom you can trust on an ongoing basis—and we hope that you have someone like that now in your life. Now, in this Transition stage, it's time to widen the circle of people who can help you. You need to find others you can trust on an ongoing basis who know about your progress, about your relapses, about what's going on with you on a regular, even a daily, basis.

Finding and Working with a Good Therapist

In the previous chapter, we strongly urged you to speak to a therapist who has expertise in this area. We again urge you to do so because we firmly believe that in order to manage this problem, you will need the help of an experienced therapist.

Once you have begun seeing a therapist, it's important to understand that there is a difference between going to therapy and actually being in therapy. "Going to therapy" means minimal involvement. It's basically showing up, sitting down, and waiting for the therapist to take charge. You don't voluntarily open up, share problems, or take any initiative. "Being in therapy," however, means that you come to each session with concerns and issues to work on. You have a commitment to being there mentally and emotionally, not just physically. You're there to take charge and to take responsibility for what happens. Therapy is not something your therapist "does" to you. Rather than resisting therapy, acknowledge your need for help. Open yourself up to the struggle and pain involved in recovery rather than trying to do everything you can to avoid it.

Once your therapist has helped you contain your behaviors, he or she can help you begin to look at the deeper issues that lie behind your compulsive and addictive behaviors, such as family-of-origin experiences, past trauma, and your relationship with others. Since working in therapy is a Second Order process, this task will take time.

Making Social Connections

Reestablishing social connections is one of the most important steps you can take in recovery, particularly if you have problems with sexual behavior on the Internet. If you've been involved in cybersex, your social relationships have atrophied to the point where you have only one, and that's between you and your computer. Although there are some useful ways to find support and to develop and refine recovery through use of the Internet, if that's as far as you take recovery, it means that your primary relationship is still between you and a computer. You must begin to develop face-to-face contacts with other human beings, and the only way to do so is through actual social activities. Enroll in a photography or foreign-language class, join a church group or bike club, volunteer at a community organization, or find other opportunities to meet people. One of the keys to breaking your link with the Internet is simply to be with other people. You need to have real, as opposed to virtual, interactions and relationships, though making them may at first be more difficult than making "virtual" relationships. You need to be out in the world interacting with other people rather than sitting at home, isolated and alone with your computer. Through these social experiences, you'll discover opportunities for deeper relationships in your life. Developing good social support can, in fact, be just as important and effective for your recovery as finding a good therapist.

Involving Family and Friends

It's important to seek support from as many places as possible. Some people are comfortable talking with others in their life, such as appropriate colleagues, good friends, and family members, while others find it enormously difficult to tell even one person. Those in the former group, however, have the best chance of achieving successful recovery.

In deciding which people in your life to talk to, use caution. Find one or two people you can truly trust, get a sponsor, contact a good therapist, and then, with the help of this support group, slowly decide whom else you should include. Over time, you will find that the more people you can include in your support group, the stronger your recovery will be.

When you begin to talk about your life, however, you will find that there are some people who don't really need to know what you have been through. Hearing your story would be painful and difficult for them. Hence, you need to respect the needs of other people and to think about the consequences of revealing your story to them. Also, it may not be appropriate to tell your co-workers or your boss, if for no other reason than that you may be fired. It may also not be appropriate to tell your parents or other extended family members.

At some point, it will be very important to involve your spouse or partner in your recovery, since his or her participation will dramatically increase your chances of success. When, how, and what should you tell your spouse or partner? The answers to these questions are difficult, and they vary for each couple. This situation presents a perfect example of why working with a therapist is so important. Together, you and your therapist can decide how to talk with your spouse or partner about these issues. The input of a professional therapist at this time will help both you and your partner better navigate these potentially treacherous waters. It's also important that your partner have a therapist, too, and that you, your partner, and both your therapists be involved in this process, especially to have help in determining how much detail you reveal to others.

Spiritual Development

Spiritual growth and development is an individual matter. How you pursue the spiritual aspects of your life can involve a variety of means, including meditation, membership in a religious organization, exploring Eastern spirituality, or practicing yoga, to name just a few. Involving someone as a spiritual coach or mentor can be useful, as can joining a spiritual community with which you can readily identify. Your spiritual growth can become a tremendous source of support for your recovery.

Twelve Step Support Groups

One proven path to recovery, though by no means the only one, is the Twelve Steps of Alcoholics Anonymous. Many people suffering from compulsive disorders have translated the Steps for their own use, including groups such as Overeaters Anonymous, Gamblers Anonymous, and Emotions Anonymous. This book proposes the Twelve Steps as one way for people with problematic sexual behavior to emerge from their double lives. Across the country, local groups have modified the Twelve Steps for the sexually compulsive. The Twelve Steps of Alcoholics Anonymous Adapted for Sexual Addicts is listed in the appendix.

Twelve Step programs can help people restore the living network of human relationships, especially in the family.

The program asks those with compulsive or addictive sexual behaviors to first accept their problem by looking at their addiction cycle and its consequences. Step One of the Twelve Steps requires individuals to take responsibility for the fact that they have a problem with cybersex and that they cannot recover from this problem without help from others. They must admit that they are powerless over their sexual behavior and that their lives have become unmanageable as a result. With that admission, individuals are then able to start rebuilding relationships by taking responsibility for what they have done and by making amends where possible. Values and priorities are reclaimed. Throughout the program, members explore basic spiritual issues as a way of understanding and facing their anxiety. As members live by the program's tenets, the double life, with all its delusion and pain, can be left behind.

Choosing a Twelve Step Group

As with all groups, some Twelve Step groups are better than others. The good ones are welcoming and supportive; they have members who have a solid recovery, and there are people in them with whom you can connect and relate. But it takes time to see these qualities. We recommend that you attend a given group at least once a week for six to eight weeks before you make a decision about whether a group is right for you.

If you feel that a given group isn't helping you or that it's not a good group for you, answer these questions before you make a final decision:

- What is it specifically that I don't like about the group?
- Do I play a part in what I don't like? If so, what part?
- What benefits am I receiving from this group?
- Are there other groups that I could go to?

It's also common for people who are new in recovery to attend meetings and come away with negative attitudes because they're still stuck in their addictive thinking. Always ask yourself whether it is "my addiction" that's doing the talking and resisting.

If, however, you are attending a Twelve Step group that discourages you from seeing a therapist or taking medications, be wary. Effective and supportive Twelve Step groups will encourage you to find and use as many sources of help as possible. If you think that therapy or medication or groups are not working for you, be careful, too! Again, this may be your addiction talking, and this is exactly why it's so important to have other people in your life who can help you see more clearly. Go to one of these people and discuss your concerns. He or she will help you make a wiser and more thoughtful decision than you could have made at this point on your own.

In the best of all worlds, you would attend one support group meeting a week (one organized by your therapist, perhaps), one group therapy meeting a week, one Twelve Step meeting a week, and an individual therapy appointment at least once every two weeks. There may be reasons why this would not be possible—lack of money, for instance. But at the very least, take one of these steps and be consistent with it.

In addition to finding and working with a good therapist, reestablishing social connections, exploring your spirituality, and involving family and friends in your recovery), here are other proven aids to recovery:

Using Your Sponsor

In chapter 4, we spoke about the crucial role your sponsor can play in your recovery. There is a big difference between simply finding a sponsor and *using* a sponsor. "Finding a sponsor" is merely the act of connecting with someone who will agree to sponsor you. Your connections are brief and somewhat perfunctory; you don't really ask for help and you don't take advantage of all that a sponsor can do for you.

"Using your sponsor" means connecting with a person who is willing to know everything about you—the whole dark side, the below-the-surface part of the volcano. Once you have a sponsor, allow this person to help you. Having and using a sponsor is about letting yourself be known. You must be willing to surrender to feedback regarding what it will take to get your life under control. And that means you have to let this person know how bad things really are right now, so he or she can see how best to help you.

Finding and Attending a Support Group

As with therapy and sponsorship, there's a difference between going to group and using a group. If you are forcing the group members to work to get through to you, if you're trying to keep as much of your life as hidden as you can, then you're just "going to group." "Using your group" requires that you let down the barriers and allow others to know who you really are. This includes sharing when you're in trouble, taking chances, trusting the group, and asking for help.

Attending Meetings

As stated previously, many people have found tremendous support for recovery from a variety of compulsive and addictive behaviors—problems with alcohol, other drugs, bulimia, gambling, sex, and more—through attending Twelve Step meetings. As with support groups, you can go to meetings and just sit in a corner and people will pretty much leave you alone. Or you can go to meetings, listen, introduce yourself, socialize with people afterward, tell your story—your *whole* story—and talk and contribute at each meeting you attend. It may take some trial and error to find a meeting that feels right for you, but when you do, make a commitment to it. Remember, you're trying to build a support network, and meetings are a great way to begin this process. These people will understand you because they have been where you are now. And they know how to help and support you because they were helped and supported by those who came before them.

Working a Program

The phrase "working a program" grew out of the Twelve Step tradition. It means to actively participate in a Twelve Step program. While Twelve Step programs can be very effective, we are using the term "program" more broadly here. By "working the program" we mean that you need to make a firm commitment to participate in whatever recovery program or process you choose. That program may differ from a Twelve Step program in that it has different assignments and goals or is behavioral oriented. Each therapy and recovery program looks a little different, but that's really not important. You could go to any number of different programs and still find help through each, as long as you are committed to the process of working that program. Conversely, you could go to the best program in the world and not be helped at all if you aren't committed. It's not so much the content of the program you attend that's critical as it is your willingness to open up and be known. Commitment to the process is the key to success. You truly need to "work" the program.

Beginning to Make Lasting Changes

At this point, you may be experiencing a range of feelings—confusion, concern, frustration, anger—and now, as you begin to look more closely at the situation you're in, feelings of loss and hopelessness. Such feelings at this point are very common. The good news, although it may be hard to believe right now, is that understanding the significance of your problem is actually the beginning of the recovery process.

In the language of Twelve Step recovery, you are beginning to take a First Step. A First Step has two critical components, the first being to acknowledge your limitations. This means admitting that you aren't the same as most other people when it comes to cybersex; you can't control your usage. The second component of a First Step is to accept that you need help with this problem and that support may come in various forms such as therapy, meditation, spiritual growth, behavioral changes, and personal exploration and growth.

We certainly are not advocating that people with compulsive or addictive cybersex behaviors become celibate for the rest of their lives. We instead want to help you find a way to develop a healthy sex life, which is much different from a life immersed in cybersex. Just as an alcoholic must stop drinking completely, so, too, must you stop your cybersex activities. Cybersex is a behavior that some people simply cannot control. There's no middle ground. Cybersex is an activity you can't take part in any longer. "Controlled" use doesn't work because it's just too easy to fall back into compulsive behaviors. There's no room for negotiation.

Alcoholics in recovery, for example, eventually come to the realization that when they drink, they just aren't like most other people. They simply can't control their alcohol use. Cybersex presents a similar problem for you, and you have to acknowledge that even though other people may be able to dabble in cybersex, you cannot. Occasional or moderate use quickly becomes an obsession. Once you accept the fact that cybersex is an activity you can't take part in at all, you will begin a grieving process.

Grieving the Loss of Cybersex

For a person with problematic cybersex behavior, sex has been the primary relationship—the main source of nurturing in life. The end of that relationship is like a death.[1] The person who stops the compulsive cybersex cycle, which gave meaning and direction to life, suffers a very real loss. Your feelings of grief will likely center around these issues: the "death" of a sexual fantasy life; the impact of past losses as a result of your cybersex behaviors; and a fear of not knowing who you'll be or what you will do without cybersex.

The Death of Your Sexual Fantasy Life

You, like many people, probably had and still have numerous sexual fantasies. When you discovered sex sites on the Internet, you soon realized that you could access any fantasy you ever had, not to mention new ones. You discovered a whole new world where you could have sex with hundreds of partners. Cybersex became the way to fulfill your dreams. But eventually you became so wrapped up in those fantasies that you lost touch with life in the real world.

Now you know that you have to let go of your cybersex life and that there are sexual limitations. Your fantasy life has taken over reality and is limiting or destroying your real relationships. By living in that fantasy world, you are actually preventing yourself from having a relationship that will be truly meaningful. And with this realization comes a profound sense of loss.

The Impact of Past Losses as a Result of Your Cybersex Behaviors

When people in recovery begin to acknowledge what's been happening to them, they look back on their lives and finally see the fallout that they've left behind—relationships that they've destroyed, botched jobs, and lost educational opportunities. The damage assessment begins, and they examine the consequences of their behavior.

Think of the time you were participating in cybersex as riding the crest of a wave that became larger as it accumulated the consequences of your behavior. But now, time has run out. The wave is coming up against the shoreline of reality and you can't pull off and paddle back out for another ride because it's simply grown too big. As the wave begins breaking, you feel all those consequences crashing down around you, tossing you like a pebble in the undertow.

Suddenly, you feel the pain of the unacknowledged losses of family, friends, job opportunities, and relationships. The embarrassment of having been discovered by a spouse, partner, or employer comes crashing through. And perhaps you are realizing just how much time you've lost doing cybersex. There may have been countless hours that could have spent enjoying friends and family, reading, taking classes, exercising, playing sports, achieving greater success and financial rewards at work, and much more.

Your grief can feel overwhelming. Since you were unaware of or denied your losses along the way, you couldn't grieve them at the time they occurred. Now they appear in front of you all at once because you've finally been able to let yourself see them.

As you become more aware of your losses, you may also feel ashamed, so much so that you may be tempted to put a barrier between you and others. While these feelings are natural and common, you should not further isolate yourself. This is, in fact, what you have been doing all along with cybersex. It's only through reconnecting with others that you will begin to heal and recover from your struggle with compulsive sexual behavior on the Internet. Recovery comes only with the support of others.

Fear of Not Knowing Who You'll Be without Cybersex

Over time, your whole identity became wrapped up in your cybersex use. Even though you knew on some level that this was unhealthy, your identity became firmly linked with your cybersex use. In a sense, it has defined who you are as a person. You grew comfortable in this identity. Cybersex became your best friend. When you were anxious or upset, it was your source of comfort. Without it, you feel lost. Shame also became part of your identity. You feel bad about what you're doing, you're incapable of stopping, and you're worried about what will take the place of cybersex and how you'll handle life without it.

Again, these feelings are a normal part of the grieving process. It's important to acknowledge and deal with them. The following signs of grief are typical in the beginning stages of recovery:

- confusion about how to act and what to do
- feelings of alienation
- fantasies about how things could have been different
- sadness over unfulfilled expectations and a wasted life
- desire for a quick fix
- feelings of exposure and vulnerability
- failure to take care of self
- uncontrollable emotions
- dark thoughts about death, including suicide
- sudden accident-prone behavior
- fear that the pain will not go away

Once you've accepted the fact that your loss of cybersex activities will cause grief, the grieving process you will go through will be similar to the process people experience when they go through other major changes or losses in life.

The grieving process has five stages. It usually begins with a ""denial" that we have actually lost something. In the second stage, called "bargaining," we partially acknowledge our loss but work hard to lessen its impact by, for example, putting the blame for the loss on others or by telling ourselves that what we lost didn't really matter to us anyway. In the third stage, we begin to feel the pain of this loss and we become "angry." Because of our pain, we may lash out at others in the hope of making ourselves feel better. Because anger doesn't really solve the problem of the loss, most people eventually move from anger into "sadness" or even "depression" as they finally accept the pain of their loss. In the final stage, called "acceptance," we begin to learn to live with our loss.

Though we have described this process in five distinct stages, the process of passing through them is not clear-cut. Often, people move back and forth between two or three stages. Even in the acceptance stage, for example, some people will occasionally feel anger and sadness. Eventually, everyone goes through a grieving process as they accept that there are limitations in their lives.

Exercise 1: The Grieving Process

The following exercise can help you work through your grieving process as you leave your cybersex behaviors behind.

A. Make a list of the cybersex behaviors you are giving up.

1. SURFING PORN SITES
2. MASTERBATING TO PORNOGRAPHY
3. USING MASTERBATION AS A COPING MECHANISM
4.
5.

Other:

B. For each behavior, describe the stage(s) of grief you are in. Tell what you are feeling or doing that signals that you are in this particular stage. For instance, are you still in denial, thinking that you don't really have to give up the behavior or that your life is just fine the way it is? Do you tell yourself that you may still be able to do this unhealthy cybersex behavior occasionally in the future because it isn't all that bad (bargaining)? Are you in the anger stage, upset about the changes in your life? Are you isolating yourself and losing sleep because of these changes (sadness)? Have you moved on and found a new way to live without this behavior (acceptance)? Remember, the stage(s) you're in may differ from one behavior to another.

BEHAVIOR: SURFING PORN SITES

Stage (or stages):

ANGER

ACCEPTANCE

BARGAINING

BEHAVIOR: MASTERBATION

Stage (or stages):

ACCEPTANCE

ANGER

BEHAVIOR: USING MASTERBATION AS A COPING MECH.

Stage (or stages):

ACCEPTANCE

BARGAINING

BEHAVIOR:

Stage (or stages):

BEHAVIOR:

Stage (or stages):

BEHAVIOR: _____

Stage (or stages):

_____

_____

_____

BEHAVIOR: _____

Stage (or stages):

_____

_____

_____

C. For each behavior, think of ways you can help yourself shift to a new stage in the grieving process.

BEHAVIOR: SURFING PORN

Ways I can help myself move ahead:

- MAKE REAL CONNECTIONS
- FIND JOY IF THEM

_____

BEHAVIOR: MASTEBAING

Ways I can help myself move ahead:

LET GO OF CHRISTIE NEEDING TO DO HER WORK

BEHAVIOR: MASTEBATION AS A COPING

Ways I can help myself move ahead:

· FIND WAYS TO CONNECT TO ME

· DO SELF SUATANG THAT IS HEALTHY

BEHAVIOR: _____

Ways I can help myself move ahead:

BEHAVIOR: _____

Ways I can help myself move ahead:

_____

_____

_____

The Twelve Steps and the Grieving Process

One resource for people struggling with out-of-control cybersex behaviors is the Twelve Step program.[2] It disrupts preoccupation and obsession with sex and supports grieving over the loss of the cybersex relationship. To make the connections explicit, we will explore each stage of the grieving process as it affects the recovering person, focusing on the help Twelve Step programs offer. The original Twelve Step program was Alcoholics Anonymous. In recent years, the Twelve Steps of AA have been adapted to help people successfully recover from other compulsive and addictive behavior, including sexual compulsivity and addiction. In the appendix, you will find the Twelve Steps of Alcoholics Anonymous adapted for Sexual Addicts, together with a Resources guide of sex addiction/compulsivity recovery programs and fellowships, including Sex Addicts Anonymous (SAA) and Sexual Compulsives Anonymous (SCA).

With all losses, bereaved people initially deny reality and isolate themselves. They resent other people who urge them to accept their loss, who would rob them of their denial. While living in denial and isolation, those with compulsive cybersex behaviors in particular deny the impact cybersex has had on their lives. Concerned friends, relatives, and professionals make an effort to confront that denial and often encounter extremely defensive behavior.

Figure 5.1   **THE LOSS OF THE CYBERSEX RELATIONSHIP**

Typical Grief Reactions to Loss of Loved Ones	Typical Grief Reactions to Loss of Cybersex Relationship	Recovery Tasks
Denial and isolation. Blame for those who press for acceptance.	Denial and isolation. Defensive about behavior.	Admission (powerlessness) and surrender (unmanageability). Acknowledge need for program.
Anger. Bargaining. Alarm reactions.	Anger and rage about loss of addiction. Slips into denial about being addict to prevent loss. Efforts to bargain. Fear of life without cybersexin an effort "Can I go on without it?"	Trust: mistrust issues worked through, including accepting Higher Power.
Acceptance of self.	Struggle to get past enormity of addictive patterns and self-degradation.	Bypass shame; increase self-acceptance.
Search for the lost relationships. Pangs of loss.	Time for slips, loss of courage, euphoric recall, testing limits.	Identify the "friends of the addict."
Emerging new identity. Reconciliation.	Pride in progress; anniversaries and straight time important.	Find comfort with new sense of self. Reconciliation with old/new friends. Restoration and forgiveness.
Establish and maintain continuity.	Integrate loss into lifestyle and behavior.	Establish network for new identity.

Step One

The First Step of the Twelve Steps helps with denial and isolation in several ways. It states: "We admitted we were powerless over our sexual addiction—that our lives had become unmanageable." Figure 5.1 summarizes the impact of losing one's relationship to cybersex.

Usually, addicts do a methodical inventory of all the ways their addiction proved to be powerful, including all those events they would have done anything to avoid but were powerless to stop. Throughout the inventory, addicts note how life has become unmanageable and intolerable with the addiction. The process helps them own their loss. They admit (to acknowledge powerlessness) and surrender (to acknowledge unmanageability) to the illness and accept their need for help. This is the process you have begun in this chapter.

Steps Two and Three

Once they have acknowledged a loss, most grieving persons become very angry. What a cybersex addict experiences is a similar feeling to when a loved one has died. Often bereaved persons feels angry with God, the deceased, and themselves for not having done more. Sometimes the anger is punctuated with moments when the bereaved bargains with God ("If only you change it, Lord, I will…") or continues to deny ("Maybe a terrible mistake has been made."). Usually the person experiences alarm or panic that reflects the terror of facing life without the loved one.

You will also become angry. You may feel angry at God for letting this happen, anger at the compulsion and addiction, anger for loss of it, and anger at yourself for not having done something sooner. Bargaining and denial ("Maybe I'm only a partial or weekend addict.") provides relief for the pain and anger. By taking the Second Step ("Came to believe a Power greater than ourselves could restore us to sanity") and the Third Step ("Made a decision to turn our will and our lives over to the care of God, as we understood Him"), you perform a significant act of trust, acknowledging a Higher Power who can help you regain sanity. You then turn your life over to your Higher Power. This leap of trust requires acceptance of the fundamental dependency of the human condition. You can then create meaning out of the experience.

Steps Four and Five

Those who suffer losses and pass through the stages of denial and anger come to accept themselves through letting go of the loved one. For those with compulsive or addictive behaviors, however, letting go does not repair all the damage the addiction has done to them. The enormity of the addictive patterns and the years of self-degradation overwhelm them. Steps Four and Five will help you bypass shame and gain self-acceptance. Step Four ("Made a searching and fearless moral inventory of ourselves") asks you to make a thorough inventory of personal strengths and weaknesses, including all the ways you have not lived up to personal values. This careful look at yourself may cause sadness and remorse.

Step Five ("Admitted to God, to ourselves, and to another human being the exact nature of our wrongs") invites you to share your inventory with another person. In sexual or cybersex recovery programs, this is usually a chaplain or pastor, although it may be another member of the fellowship. The experience of relating all that history to someone else exposes you to an extreme level of vulnerability. Being so exposed, and yet being affirmed and accepted, creates healing of the highest order. The spiritual skills of the clergy may play a key role in self-forgiveness and self-acceptance. In effect, you can feel restored to the human community. Often, great joy and relief occur after the Fifth Step has been taken.

Steps Six and Seven

As in all grief, the struggle does not subside with self-acceptance. Bereaved persons have moments during which they search intensely for the lost relationship. You will experience pangs of loss when your sadness and desire for the old way returns. This is a time for "slips," loss of courage, euphoric recall, and testing limits. Once again, the program provides a framework to help with this. Steps Six and Seven ask you to be ready to let go of the defects of character that could bring back the compulsive-addictive life. Part of letting go requires trust in a Higher Power and trust in the existence of a healing process. With Steps Six ("Were entirely ready to have God remove all these defects of character") and Seven ("Humbly asked Him to remove our shortcomings"), you identify your compulsive "friends"—those beliefs, defenses, attitudes, behaviors, and other issues that supported your addictive behavior when it flourished. For example, you may begin to recognize how self-pity serves as a gateway back into addiction. Now you know you must stop giving in to self-pity and other behaviors that supported your cybersex behavior.

Steps Eight and Nine

As the grieving process evolves, a new sense of identity emerges. With restored confidence, the bereaved seek reconciliation with people they had pushed away. For you, the renewal of identity takes concrete form in terms of celebrating your progress. Marking anniversaries (for example, at one, three, and six months, a year, two years, and so on) becomes extremely important.

Building on this renewed sense of self, your shame will no longer prevent reconciliation with friends and family. With Steps Eight ("Made a list of all persons we had harmed, and became willing to make amends to them all") and Nine ("Made direct amends to such people wherever possible, except when to do so would injure them or others"), you list those people you have harmed and make amends to them in hopes of healing the breach in the relationship. Making these direct efforts brings comfort through further restoration of self and, in some cases, forgiveness.

All who suffer great losses reach a point where they must establish their renewed identity and recognize that life goes on. It is not true, however, that when grief subsides, pain goes away entirely. In effect, although the sadness never leaves, it is transformed, becoming incorporated into our beings as part of that suffering that brings wisdom and depth of feeling to all of us. One simply learns to adjust to life in order to carry the suffering.

Steps Ten, Eleven, and Twelve

Step Ten ("Continued to take personal inventory and when we were wrong promptly admitted it)" encourages a daily effort to take stock of your life using the principles of the first nine Steps. Step Eleven ("Sought through prayer and meditation to improve our conscious contact with God as we understood Him, praying only for knowledge of His will for us and the power to carry that out") suggests that spiritual progress results from a daily effort to improve conscious contact with a Higher Power. Step Twelve ("Having had a spiritual awakening as the result of these steps, we tried to carry this message to others and to practice these principles in all our affairs") asks you to tell other addicts about the power of the program. You pass on what you have received.

These last three Steps help the integrate the program principles into daily life, and the program thus becomes an intervening system that disrupts the addictive system and provides ongoing support for the lifelong process of surviving the loss. In effect, you will join a community based on healing principles validated over time. The Twelve Steps consolidate these common principles into a discipline for living daily with suffering and loss. Although their simplicity can mislead the unknowing, these Steps require great courage and can result in profound experiences.

The Critical Importance of a First Step

Whether you are taking Step One of the Twelve Steps or simply taking your first steps in getting your cybersex behaviors under control, you must acknowledge that cybersex is a problem you will have to manage—and unless you do, severe consequences will follow. Your efforts must also go beyond merely managing the crisis stage or you will simply fall back into your destructive cybersex patterns and behaviors. These behaviors are symptoms of a deeper and more complex problem that will necessitate significant changes in your life.

Taking these first steps is not easy. It's difficult because it brings many emotions to the surface, one of which is fear of the unknown. You may wonder how you can live without cybersex, since it has been your identity and life's focus. Being worried about this admission is natural. Many other people have felt exactly the same way. Courageously, they took that First Step and eventually recovered from their compulsive or addictive behaviors to live happy and fulfilling lives.

Taking the First Step is absolutely necessary. It's a prerequisite for everything that follows. Without it, your chances of learning to manage your behavior are slim. Step

One is the foundation for future work, and until you create this foundation, none of the other Steps we will suggest will work.

Earlier in the book, we used food and eating as an analogy. In that same vein, when we are cooking, we follow a recipe, either from a cookbook or from one we keep in our memory. In most recipes, there are certain ingredients that can be manipulated or even left out altogether without substantially compromising the result. But there are other ingredients that are essential to each recipe. Step One fits in the latter category. Without Step One, the recipe for recovery will be a flop.

Yes, Step One is difficult and painful. But we want to emphasize again that it is really the beginning of recovery. It is true that life will seem worse before it feels better. But that's because you're eliminating your "medication"—the behavior you've been using to anesthetize the pain of all your losses during the time you've been doing cybersex. It has become an emotional anesthetic, hiding the pain.

If you look back, you can probably find points in your life when you started to feel some of the losses and consequences of your behavior. What did you do then? Did you turn away and flee back into cybersex behaviors? If so, what was the result? Probably nothing changed and your life just kept getting worse.

When you stop these behaviors, you experience your losses and pain. Remember, part of the goal of a First Step is to provide a safe place to begin experiencing this pain. It's OK—even necessary—to let yourself experience all the feelings that have been pent up inside you. In the end, you will feel better. This process is akin to going into a house that's been shuttered and closed for a long time and throwing open the doors and windows to let in the fresh air and sun. You are throwing open the windows on being fully human.

Rationalizations That Interfere with the First Step

We all have a natural tendency to develop rationalizations to protect ourselves from things that are frightening and painful. When we begin the grieving process, no matter the reason, it's likewise quite natural to develop certain rationalizations to protect ourselves from it.

In Step One, you will begin work on three critical recovery tasks: recognizing your powerlessness over cybersex behaviors, determining ways your life has become unmanageable because of these behaviors, and examining the consequences of these behaviors. People recovering from problematic cybersex behaviors typically experience some of the following eight rationalizations. As you begin your First Step, you will soon see just how misleading the following eight rationalizations are.

Rationalization 1: It's not real

Cyberspace isn't real. There are no people. There are no rules. There are no consequences (that are immediately apparent, at least!). I can indulge in cybersex without worrying about it.

Rationalization 2: Cybersex doesn't hurt others.

I'm not having skin-to-skin contact, so it's not sex, and it's not affecting anyone. No one can get a disease. It can't hurt anyone. I'm not unfaithful because I haven't really done anything with anybody. Even when I'm in a chat room, for example, it's all still make-believe. Most of the time, I'm not who I say I am. There is no direct harm to anybody and there isn't anything I need to be accountable for.

Rationalization 3: Cybersex doesn't hurt me.

I'm just on the computer, so what's the big deal? It's no different from surfing other kinds of Web sites on the Internet. There aren't any consequences. As long as I don't have skin-to-skin contact, I'm not hurting myself at all.

Rationalization 4: I can stop anytime I want; I just need to turn off the computer.

None of this is real, anyway. I'm not actually going to a strip club, seeing a prostitute, or exposing myself to a real person. Besides, all I need to do is shut down the computer and everything goes away.

Rationalization 5: I've already done a First Step.

I've already done a First Step for sex addiction (or for alcohol use, gambling, or another addiction), so why would I need to do another one? Besides, I've been sober for years.

Rationalization 6: Cybersex doesn't have any consequences.

I can't get a sexually transmitted disease. It's not going to destroy my marriage if no one has my mailing address or knows where I live. Using the computer is private. No one knows my access codes. When I'm online at work, well, that's no different from taking a short coffee break in the cafeteria.

Rationalization 7: It's just a game—it's virtual reality.

This isn't serious because it's not real. That's why it's called virtual reality. It's fun, it's my entertainment, and it doesn't bother or hurt anybody. Who would ever take this seriously? I don't really mean anything by any of this. It's no different from a video game.

Rationalization 8: I just use it occasionally. Cybersex doesn't interfere with or jeopardize things in my life.

I'm not on the computer all the time or anything like that. I just go on when I feel like it. It's just something to do. I'm still in a good relationship with my partner, have a good job, and spend time with my kids. It's no big deal!

Powerlessness

"Powerlessness" means being unable to stop your cybersex behaviors no matter how hard you try and despite negative consequences. Have you tried to stop, cut back, set limits on, or change the types of your use?

You may, for example, have promised yourself you wouldn't use your computer at work for cybersex, especially after your information services department began monitoring Internet use, yet you continued to do so despite the danger. You might have promised yourself you'd never go to a particular sexual Web site again, but you ended up at a similar one. You may have promised yourself that you'd never stay online past 11:00 p.m. to engage in cybersex activities, but you found yourself online in the middle of the night at least three nights a week.

Consider how much you have been preoccupied with cybersex and how much you have been using it as a way to reduce anxiety in your life. How have your thinking and activities revolved around your cybersex use? Planning your day around your use, daydreaming about when you'll be free to participate in cybersex, and becoming anxious and angry when situations arise that prevent you from using are examples of preoccupation and powerlessness.

It's also important to note that any attempt to control your cybersex behavior is an indication that it is already out of control.

Exercise 2: Powerlessness Inventory

In the space below or on a separate sheet of paper, begin your powerlessness inventory. List examples that show how powerless you have been to stop your Internet sexual behavior. Be explicit about types of behavior and frequency. Start with your earliest example of being powerless and conclude with your most recent. Write down as many examples as you can think of. By doing so, you will see the pattern of broken promises emerge and add significantly to the depth of your understanding of your powerlessness over these behaviors.

1. WANTED TO STOP SURFING PORN SITES AFTER

   GETTING MARRIED : CANCELED ONE SUBSCRIPTION BUT STARTED
   ANOTHER 3-4 MONTHS AFTER

2. _____

   _____

3. _____

   _____

4. _____

_____

5. _____

_____

6. _____

_____

7. _____

_____

8. _____

_____

Unmanageability

Unmanageability and powerlessness are closely intertwined. Unmanageability is, in fact, the manifestation of powerlessness. When you lose the ability to control your cybersex behavior, it affects all aspects of your life and soon becomes unmanageable. "Unmanageability" means that your cybersex use has created chaos and damage in your life. These are the consequences of powerlessness.

Al's story is a poignant example of unmanageability:

> One night I finally realized what I'd been doing to my kids. I was in my home office on the computer when my two children came in and wanted to play. I screamed at them to shut up and go find something else to do and to leave me alone. When I turned back to the screen, it finally hit me. I was screaming at my own children to leave so I could have cybersex. I finally saw the impact of my addiction and how it was affecting my relationship with them. I wasn't asking them to leave me alone so I could work or to prepare for a meeting or a community activity. No, I was saying, in effect, "Leave me alone because I'm having sex on the Internet."

Use the space at right to list how your life has become unmanageable as a result of your cybersex behaviors.

Exercise 3: Unmanageability Inventory

1. NOT ENOUGH SLEEP

2. SICK

3. LOW ENERGY @ WORK

4. DISTRACTED

5. LIXING IN SHAME

6.

7.

8.

Facing the Consequences

Most people with compulsive or addictive behaviors have some expectation that everyone will overlook the damage caused by what they do. Some become indignant when they do experience consequences—getting fired, bouncing checks, or being arrested, for example.

Consequences, however, are signposts to reality. You receive them because the world does not share your distortion of reality. Lies, broken promises, and exploitive behavior will eventually cost, and cost dearly.

It's extremely useful to do a complete inventory of the consequences of your cybersex behaviors. All people who have experienced out-of-control sexual behavior, used sex to cope with stress, or acted out sexually have experienced the consequences of their behavior. When you stop and really look at the results of your cybersex behavior, you will see for the first time just how you and many others have been affected in a variety of different ways.

Exercise 4: The Effects of Cybersex

Read and answer each of the following questions honestly. Spend as much time as you need to complete this exercise. Later, you may want to share your answers with others who are helping you in recovery, such as your sponsor or therapist.

A. SOCIAL LIFE
Consider how your cybersex behaviors have affected your social life.

- Loss of important friendships.
- Loss of interest in hobbies or activities.
- Few friends (or no friends) who don't participate in or condone your sexual behavior.
- Becoming isolated from family and friends.
- Spending so much time online that you're too tired to take part in other social activities.

List three specific examples of how your cybersex behaviors have affected your social life.

1. FEW FRIENDS

2. TIRED

3. _____

3. _____

_____

B. PHYSICAL CONDITION
Consider the effect your cybersex behaviors have had on you physically.

- Continuation of addictive behavior despite the risk to your health.
- Extreme weight loss or gain.
- Physical problems, such as ulcers or high blood pressure.
- Physical injury or abuse by others.
- Involvement in potentially abusive or dangerous situations.
- Vehicle accidents (automobile, motorcycle, bicycle).
- Injury to yourself from your sexual behavior.
- Sleep disturbances (not enough sleep, too much sleep).
- Lack of energy/physical exhaustion.

List three examples of how your cybersex behaviors have affected your physical condition.

1. WEIGHT GAIN _____

_____

2. NOT ENOUGH SLEEP _____

_____

3. LACK OF ENERGY _____

_____

C. ECONOMIC IMPACT

Consider the effect your cybersex behaviors have had on your financial condition.

- Overspending.
- Loss of job or job promotions.
- Mismanagement of household funds.

List three examples of how your cybersex behaviors have affected you economically.

1. NO PROMOTION

2. NO DISCRETIONARY FUNDS (MANAGED BY CHRISTIE)

3.

D. JOB OR PROFESSION

Consider the effect cybersex behaviors have had on your work and career.

- ✱ Lowered productivity.
- ✱ Frequent absenteeism.
- ✱ Deteriorating quality of product or decision-making.
- ✱ Frequent tardiness.
- Demotion at work.
- ✱ Loss of co-workers' respect.
- Loss of the opportunity to work in the career of your choice.
- Loss of educational opportunities.
- Loss of business.
- Forced to change careers.
- ✱ Not working to your level of capability.
- Termination from job.

List three examples of how your cybersex behaviors have affected your work and career.

1. _____

_____

2. _____

_____

3. _____

_____

E. SCHOOL

If you are a student, consider the impact your cybersex behaviors have had on your education.

- Not keeping up with homework assignments.
- Dropped classes and incompletes.
- Frequent absenteeism.
- Low or failing grades.
- Social isolation.

List three examples of how your cybersex behaviors have affected your social activities or education.

1. SOCIAL ISOLATION _____

_____

2. _____

_____

3. _____

_____

F. EMOTIONAL PROBLEMS

Consider how your cybersex use has affected you emotionally.

- Feelings of hopelessness and despair.
- Difficulty in getting close to others or in expressing feelings.
- Extreme feelings of loneliness and isolation.
- Unexplained fears.
- Thoughts of suicide.
- Attempted suicide.
- Homicidal thoughts or feelings.
- Feeling like you had two different lives—one public and one secret.
- Depression, paranoia, or fear of going insane.
- Loss of touch with reality.
- Loss of self-esteem.
- Acting against your own values and beliefs.
- Strong feelings of guilt and shame.
- Emotional exhaustion.

List three examples of how your cybersex behaviors have affected you emotionally.

1. Used CyberSex as a way of not confronting Christie

2. Had to lie about Cybersex use, made Christie feel that I didn't like it

3.

G. FAMILY PROBLEMS

Consider how your cybersex behaviors have interfered with relationships that mean the most to you.

- Loss of closeness.
- A feeling that other family members have lost respect for you.
- Using family members emotionally or financially.
- Extreme feelings of remorse or guilt.
- Withdrawing from family activities.
- Increase in marital or relationship problems.
- Being unfaithful to your partner or spouse.
- Risking the loss of partner or spouse.
- Loss of partner or spouse.
- Jeopardizing the well-being of your family.

List three examples of how your cybersex behaviors have affected your closest relationships.

1. Would feel guilty about using cybersex afterwards

2. Cybersex was cheating on Christie

3. Risked my marrge

H. SPIRITUAL PROBLEMS

Finally, consider how your cybersex use has affected you spiritually.

- Having vague spiritual desires but no spiritual direction.
- A sense that life has no meaning.
- A feeling of emptiness.
- Moving from belief to agnosticism/atheism as addiction progresses.
- Becoming upset at or hostile toward any reference to religion or religious beliefs.
- Staying away from church because of guilt feelings.
- Feeling abandoned by God or your Higher Power.
- Feeling anger at God or your Higher Power.
- Loss of faith in anything spiritual.

List three examples of how your cybersex behaviors have affected you spiritually.

1. EMPTINESS _____

_____

2. ANGER _____

_____

3. HOSTILE AT REFERENCE TO RELIGION _____

_____

Until now, when you've thought about your cybersex behaviors, you've tended to ignore any potential consequences. You stopped at the point of your gratification. Now that you've begun to examine the consequences of your cybersex activities, we want you to carry out the scenario to its true conclusion—one that includes the consequences to you and to the other people affected by your behavior.

Liz's story is a good example:

After a big promotion, my husband began working very long hours, leaving me with an increased burden of care for our three young children, ages six, eight, and twelve. He'd leave early each morning and often arrive home at 8:00 or 9:00 p.m. He was also away from home for extended periods of work-related travel. After a few months, we decided to hire a nanny to help me care for the children. As more time passed, I became depressed. One day, I discovered chat rooms on the Internet and became instantly hooked. The ones I got involved with were interesting and there was a lot of flirting and sexual talk. It was like an interactive soap opera. Well, I started spending huge amounts of time online and was having a great time. Everything there seemed so alive and exciting. It took me a long time to realize that I was completely ignoring my children. When they'd come to me for something, I'd invariably be on the computer and would tell them to ask the nanny. I left all their care to her. And I was ignoring my husband during the little time he was home. The kids were starting to act out in school, something that had never happened before, and their grades were slipping. Eventually I met a man online who seemed very attractive. Then I did something I swore I'd never do—I agreed to meet him at a local motel. I thought that this was the man of my dreams. The evening was a disaster—essentially I was brutalized by him, and there was nothing I could do about it because, as it turned out, his name and identity were completely false.

Exercise 5: Describe One of Your Cybersex Experiences

To help you better see yourself and your cybersex behaviors, we now ask you to write about one of your cybersex experiences—and carry it far enough that you include the consequences that resulted from your behavior.

As a way of Relieving Stress, and sexaul tension
I masterbated to club jenna, com 1/2x a month
I thought that I deserved to be able to
surf porn a masterbate because my wife was too
tired to have sex with me. I would go down
stairs after she was asleep. I went to the web
site, picked out a video, and started to masterbate
until I had an orgasm

When I was done, I went up stairs and as quietly as possible (because I was ashamed) cleaned up and changed my clothes a went to Bed

A couple of weeks later, Christie found a charge on our check card for the web site. She went to the website and found out it was a porn site. She became very upset and started to cry. I thought our marge was over

Denying the Consequences of Cybersex Behavior

For a long time, Liz was in denial about the effects her cybersex behaviors were having. Denial, of course, can be an honest, straightforward disagreement or refusal. When coupled with out-of-control sexual behavior, however, denial becomes a potent and powerful way of protecting oneself from discovery—and from help.

Denial is the confused kind of thinking and reasoning used to avoid the reality of behavior or consequences of behavior.[3] It is a way to try to manage and explain the chaos in your life. It is an effort to protect cybersex behavior you believe you can't live without. It is a way to deflect attention and responsibility. Here are some examples of excuses that represent denial:

- "It was only once in awhile."
- "No one was hurt because no one knows."
- "I needed to get my needs met somewhere."
- "We are all adults."
- "I am just being a man (woman)."
- "If you think I'm bad, you should see so-and-so."
- "My situation is different."

Exercise 6: Denial's Role in Your Life

Let's look at what role denial is playing in your life. List all of the reasons you believed—or maybe still believe—you don't belong in therapy or a group for your cybersex behaviors.

1. Lots of people use pornography.

2. I never had a problem, I only used cybersex occasionally

3. I have the right to make myself feel good

4. If my wife was more sexual, I wouldn't have this problem

5. I could control it

6. _____

7. _____

8. _____

9. _____

10. _____

11. _____

12. _____

13. _____

14. _____

15. _____

There are many kinds of denial. A few of the primary categories are listed below. Beneath each of them there is room for you to write your own examples.

Global thinking: Attempting to justify that something is not a problem by using terms like "always" or "never" or by saying "People always use the Net, that's why."

"Lots of people", Everyone is doing it

_____

_____

Rationalization: Justifying unacceptable behavior. "I don't have a problem—I'm just sexually liberated." "You people are such prudes!" "You're crazy."

Since others do it can't be all that bad

_____

_____

Minimizing: Trying to make behavior or consequences seem smaller and less important than they are. "Only a little." "Only once in awhile." "It is no big deal."

_____

_____

_____

Comparison: Shifting the focus to someone else to justify behaviors. "I'm not as bad as _____."

I am not a sex addict. I was not Compusive like the guys in SA.

_____

_____

Uniqueness: Thinking you are different or special. "My situation is different." "I was hurt more." "That's fine for you, but I'm too busy to go to group right now."

I have been to therapy so I can handle it

_____

_____

Avoiding by creating an uproar or distraction: Being a clown and getting everyone laughing; angry outbursts meant to frighten; threats and posturing; shocking behavior that may or may not be sexual.

_____

_____

_____

Avoiding by omission: Trying to change the subject, ignore the subject, or manipulate the conversation to avoid talking about something. It is also leaving out important bits of information, like the fact that a lover is sixteen or that it's your friend's partner.

_____

_____

_____

Blaming: "Well, you would cruise all night, too, if you had my job." "If my wife/husband/partner weren't so cold, I wouldn't have to have an affair." "I can't help it—the baby cries day and night and makes me nervous."

__if Christe was more sexaul..._____

_____

_____

Intellectualizing: Avoiding feelings and responsibility by thinking or by asking why. Explaining everything. Getting lost in detail and storytelling. Pretending superior intellect and using intelligence as a weapon.

__I am smart enough to control it_____

_____

_____

Hopelessness/helplessness: "I'm a victim; I can't help it." "There is nothing I can do to get better." "I'm the worst."

__I have to maisterbate._____

_____

_____

Manipulative behavior: Usually involves some distortion of reality including the use of power, lies, secrets, or guilt to exploit others.

If I am angry I should be able to do it

our neighbor did it

Compartmentalizing: Dividing your life into "compartments" so that you can keep various parts separate from one another.

I said one thing (Porn is bad) but lived another life

Crazy-making: When confronted by people who do have a correct perception, telling them they are totally wrong and being indignant that they would think such a thing. This encourages them to believe that they are "crazy," that they cannot trust their own perceptions.

Seduction: The use of charm, humor, good looks, or helpfulness to gain sexual access and cover up insincerity.

Exercise 7: Creating a Personal Narrative

Now that you have gained more awareness of your life, particularly your cybersex behaviors, we would like you to take some time to write a personal narrative. This will be similar to your own "case study," but more extensive. We want you to tell your cybersex story. How did you get started? What led you to it? What did you find attractive about it? How did your behaviors increase? What activities did you engage in? What were you feeling and thinking during all this? You may find it useful to refer to the cybersex log you created in chapter 1, as well as to other exercises in this and previous chapters.

Here's one additional guideline: Write this narrative in the third person. Refer to yourself by your own name in this narrative. In other words, if your name is Joe, then you might begin as follows:

Joe, a thirty-seven-year-old manager in a small manufacturing company, . . .

Use additional paper if you need to. Be thorough. Be sure to include consequences of your behaviors, too.

Write your story here:

WHEN I WAS SEVEN/8 I WANTED TO KNOW MORE ABOUT SEX. I SAW FLASHES ON TV FROM BLOCKED SHOWS AND I COULD HEAR THE SOUND. I STARTED SEEKING OUT PORN MAGAZINES AND MASTERBATED TO THE IMAGES AT NIGHT. I HID THE MAGAZINES UNDER MY BED, BUT MY MOM FOUND THEM. WHEN SHE DID, SHE CONFRONTED ME WITH THEM IN FRONT OF MY DAD, BUT HE DIDN'T DO ANYTHING BUT GLANCE THROUGH THEM. AFTER THAT I BECAME MORE CAREFUL AND SECRETIVE, BUT ALSO ESCALATED MY CHOICES FOR MORE EXPLICIT PORN.

AGAIN, IN COLLEGE, MY ROOMMATE SUSPECTED I WAS USING PORN TO SEXUALLY SATISFY MYSELF AND I CARRIED SHAME AROUND THAT. BUT DIDN'T STOP. WHEN I HAD A G.F. IN COLLEGE I STOPED BUYING/USING PORN UNTIL THE RELATIONSHIP ENDED. AFTER COLLEGE I STARTED BUYING/WATCHING VIDEOS, BUT WHEN I STARTED USING THE INTERNET, I WOULD JUST DOWNLOAD THEM. I NEVER STARTED COLLECTING THE PORN, AND WOULD ONLY THROW IT OUT IF I THOUGHT IT WOULD BE DISCOVERED.

WHEN MY WIFE SAW THE PORN SITE CHARGE ON OUR BILLING STATEMENT AND CONFRONTED ME, I FINALLY ADMITED AND STOPED.
I HAVE BEEN SOBER SINCE ... AND IN TREATMENT.

When you finish your story, take a break. Wait for a day or so, and then come back and read what you've written. Then continue by answering the following questions.

Now that you've written your story, what are your feelings about it?

SHORTER

NOT AS MUCH SHAME

MORE ESCALATION IN IT THAN I THOUGHT

Are you surprised at what's there? If so, in what ways?

ESCALATION

REASONS FOR BEHAVIOR

GETTING CAUGHT ONLY SLOWED ME DOWN BEFORE

Were you aware of what was really going on in your life? If not, why do you think you weren't?

NO

I WAS LIVING IN A DREAM WORLD, WHERE I

COULD HAVE SEX WHENEVER I NEEDED N

What parts weren't you aware of?

TIME, AND HOW COMPULSIVE I WAS

Does the person in your narrative seem like a stranger to you? If so, in what way?

YES, YOUNGER AND NOT SURE OF HIMSELF

Do you think this is how other people see you? Why or why not?

ONCE THEY DID, NOW I AM NOT SURE

Accepting Yourself

Your admission of powerlessness and unmanageability marks the beginning of your recovery. You must now take the next step of acceptance—acceptance that your behavior has been compulsive—and that you need ongoing help to achieve freedom from the power of cybersex.

When you finally take time to really look at your behaviors, the result can be shocking. You're probably saying to yourself, "So I have this problem and it's out of control. What can I do? How can I get my life back together?" Regardless of your worries, take heart, because you are now on the road to recovery from these behaviors.

Recognizing False Rationalizations

Earlier in this chapter, we presented eight rationalizations that are commonly used to deny or excuse problematic online sexual behaviors. The following four explanations substitute reality for those rationalizations.

Rationalization 1: They're just electrons; they're not real. They're only "virtual."

Regardless of the "unreality" of the Internet, real people are involved. You're real. The other people online are real, even if you can't really see or touch them. Your family is real. Your colleagues are real. Your children are real. Your behavior affects real human beings.

Rationalization 2: Cybersex doesn't hurt others, it doesn't hurt me, and there are no consequences.

Just looking at the lists you made of the consequences of your cybersex behaviors should put these illusions to rest.

Rationalization 3: Occasional use isn't a problem for me. Besides, I can stop anytime I want. I just need to turn off the computer.

You probably often told yourself this, but did you stop? Did you turn off the computer? Did "occasional" use become "using whenever I had the opportunity"? Were you able to stop? And even when you did, did the fantasies stop spinning in your head? How about the desire to go back online? If you could have stopped whenever you wanted, you would have. But you didn't because you couldn't stop.

Rationalization 4: I've already done a First Step; why do another for this?

Regardless of other First Steps you may have done, it is imperative that you do a First Step that focuses on cybersex so that you can recognize powerlessness, unmanageability, and consequences in terms of this particular behavior.

Recognizing When You're in Danger of Relapse

Relapses are very common during the Transition stage. Having passed through the crisis stage, people now begin to realize that recovery will require much more time, energy, and emotional involvement than they had thought. It is very important at this stage to recognize that you are at a typical point of relapse. Because of this, we are offering you the following information and exercises to help you better recognize when you are in danger of a relapse and to know what to do to prevent it.

Relapses tend to be seen as a matter of impulse—as a moment of weakness when someone lets down his or her guard. Research has shown us, however, that this is not the case. Stress, coping strategies (or lack thereof), and decision-making skills all play a role, as do "SUDS"—seemingly unimportant decisions.[4] Relapse is really the culmination of a chain of events that starts days, weeks, or even months in advance of its actual occurrence. Often, the actual relapse act can't be carried out immediately because of situational constraints such as, in the case of cybersex, unavailability of computer and Internet access or the lack of privacy. The desire for immediate gratification may be temporarily put off and instead be redirected to secret planning or fantasies about cybersex. Because of the potential for conflict and guilt associated with these secret schemes and plans, people are likely to engage in rationalization or denial, or both. These two distorted ways of thinking can then combine to influence certain choices or decisions as part of a chain of events leading ultimately to a relapse.

We believe that people who are headed for a relapse make a number of minor decisions over time, each of which brings them a bit closer to the brink of the triggering high-risk situation. An example is the abstinent drinker who buys a bottle of sherry to take home, "just in case guests drop by." Or the ex-smoker who decides it would be fine to choose a seat in the smoking section of a restaurant. Or the recovering gambler who expands a vacation driving trip to California to include a visit to Lake Tahoe, which is just a few miles down the road from the gambling mecca of Reno, Nevada.

The term "SUDS" (seemingly unimportant decisions) describes these decisions. It is as though people slowly begin to set the stage for a possible relapse by making a series of SUDS, each of which moves them one step closer to relapse. A final advantage in "setting up" a relapse in this way is that people may be able to avoid assuming responsibility for the relapse episode itself. By putting themselves in an extremely tempting high-risk situation, they can claim that they were "overwhelmed" by external circumstances that made it "impossible" to resist the relapse.

Stress can be a powerful relapse trigger, too—one that should not be underestimated. Consider this scenario: Over the past few weeks, one of your children has been having problems at school. This has taken extra time from you and your spouse. In addition, your spouse has been worrying about an impending visit from her parents. The result: There's a lot more tension around your house than normal, and it's been building up for a few weeks, wearing you down. You've been thinking more and more about how good it would be to go online for a little dose of cybersex, just like old times. You've resisted this temptation with the help of your sponsor. But now it's Friday evening, you're at home by yourself—and your computer is readily available.

One of your primary relapse prevention goals is to become aware of the behavior chains that can lead you to relapse. If you can recognize them, then you can take action long before you get to the point of relapse. In the example above, talking with your wife about the stress you're feeling and your concerns about the end result would be a positive step in breaking the chain. Once you recognize your behavior chain, you can begin planning ways to substitute new, positive, and supportive behaviors to prevent relapse. You realize that when life gets stressful at home, you need to spend time with a friend, for example, or talk with your wife about it, or get some exercise. Essentially, you need to do whatever seems to help relieve the stress before you feel the need to turn to cybersex for relief.

The concept of behavior chains and our power to change them points out an important difference between a First Order and a Second Order relapse. People who have First Order relapses always think that the cause of the relapse is something outside of themselves. The cause is external, something over which they have no control. They might say, for example, that it was their spouse's nagging that caused the relapse, or an argument with a relative, or a boss who was pressuring them. On the other hand, people who have made Second Order changes would talk about this relapse in terms of their own responsibility: "I have been fighting with my wife a lot lately" or "I haven't really been responsible at work lately." These people realize that they are responsible for their behavior.

Behavior chains and our power to change them also shows the importance of identifying your relapse triggers and determining ways to avoid them. We already have numerous procedures in our society that require us to prepare for the possibility (no matter how remote) that various dangerous situations may arise. For example, fire drills help us be prepared in case a fire breaks out in public buildings or schools. Certainly no one believes that requiring people to participate in fire drills increases the probability of future fires; on the contrary, the aim is actually to minimize the extent of personal loss and damage should a fire happen. The same logic applies in the case of relapse prevention.

Behavior Chains: What Leads You to Cybersex?

Engaging in cybersex is preceded by a series of thoughts and events that lead up to it. The following exercise will help you identify the behavior chains that lead you to cybersex.

In the exercise (page 150), you'll see a series of boxes. The last box contains the words "cybersex behavior." Your goal in doing this exercise is to determine what behaviors and thoughts lead you to a particular cybersex behavior, beginning with the behavior just before the episode, and working backward as far as you can.

For example, just previous to your cybersex episode, you might have clicked on to a porn Web site. You'd write that in the second to the final box. Before that, it might be logging on to the Net. Before that, you began to think about cybersex. Before that, you had a fight with your spouse or partner. Before that, you were feeling tense and anxious. Before that, you were given a difficult assignment by your manager at work. And so on.

At this point, you might not be able to track backwards more than four or five steps. Don't be concerned if that's the case. As you progress in your recovery, you'll find that you'll become much more clear about what has led up to your cybersex behaviors. In a month or two, you might find it interesting to come back to this exercise and see if you can add to these chains.

Exercise 8: My Behavior Chains

	BORED
	DECIDE TO GO ON CPU
	RUN OUT OF NON PORN THINGS TO DO
	CLICK ON PORN SITE
	cybersex behavior VIEW VIDEO AND SELF SOOTHE

	cybersex behavior

cybersex behavior

Exercise 9: Intervention Cards

Now that you have gained some knowledge about what leads to your cybersex behaviors, you can do something about interrupting that chain by making "intervention cards." First, you need some three-by-five-inch index cards. Then, follow these steps:

1. On the front of one card, write down the behaviors in one of the chains you completed in the previous exercise. Begin with the behavior immediately preceding your cybersex episode.

2. On the reverse side, write down a consequence that corresponds to each of those behaviors.

When you're finished, each behavior on the front side of your card should have a corresponding consequence on the back side. If you have five behaviors, you need to have five consequences.

Here's an example:

FRONT SIDE

Behaviors:

1. Logged on to a porn site and acted out.

2. Logged on to the Net when no one else was home.

3. Picked a fight with my wife.

4.

5.

BACK SIDE

Consequences:

1. Felt ashamed of myself.

2. Increased the likelihood that I'd go to a sex site.

3. Felt greater emotional distance from wife; created

   more tense atmosphere.

4.

5.

Next, take a second index card. On the front of this one, make a list of the actions you could take to avoid your cybersex behavior.

On the reverse side of the card, write the benefits you receive from these actions.

FRONT SIDE

Behaviors:
1. Call my sponsor when feeling the urge for cybersex.
2. When no one is home, go outside for a long walk or bike ride. Call a friend.
3. Talk calmly with my wife about my difficult day and my worries.

BACK SIDE

Benefits:
1. Avoided relapse into cybersex! Feel good about myself and my recovery.
2. Reduced stress; feel much more calm.
3. Improved communication with my wife; increased our feelings of togetherness.

When you've completed a set of cards for each behavior chain, put them in your wallet, briefcase, or purse so that they will be at your fingertips when you need to refer to them. When you become aware that you are in one of your cybersex chains, pull out your cards and go over them. You'll immediately remind yourself of the consequence of this impending behavior, as well as an alternative to it and the benefits you'll reap if you choose the alternative. Intervention cards are a great tool for helping people make healthier choices. Often, just knowing that you have the cards with you is enough to help you avoid cybersex.

Exercise 10: Relapse Drill

You may also want to include this "relapse drill" as part of your prevention strategy. Learning precise prevention skills and related strategies is more helpful than relying on vague suggestions to "work your program."

To begin, think of situations that you know could trigger a relapse for you. (You may want to refer to the Relapse Prevention Worksheet, exercise 4 in chapter 4, to help you with this exercise and the above Intervention Card exercise.) Start with the scenarios that would be less likely to lead to relapse, and then move on to ones that would place you at higher risk until, finally, you list the situation that would be the most dangerous for you. Then, for each of these situations, think of ways you could react that would enable you to escape the "fire" without being burned. As the intensity and risk of relapse increases with each situation, your escape plan will need to be better thought out. List six or more relapse-threatening situations.

POTENTIAL RELAPSE SITUATIONS

Low risk

1. GOING ON-LINE AFTER WATCHING A MOVIE WITH SEXUAL CONTENT

Escape behaviors: _____

_____

_____

_____

2. GOING ONLINE WHILE ON VACATION AND ALONE

Escape behaviors: _____

_____

_____

_____

3. GOING ONLINE AFTER SEX

Escape behaviors: _____

_____

_____

_____

Moderate risk

1. STAYING ON LINE AFTER 11:00 PM

Escape behaviors: _____

_____

_____

_____

2. READING EMAIL WITH SEXAUL CONTENT

Escape behaviors: _____

_____

_____

_____

3. _____

Escape behaviors: _____

_____

_____

_____

High risk

1. STAYING ON A PAY SEX SITE AFTER
   CLICKING ON IT.

Escape behaviors: _____

_____

_____

2. WATCHING A SEX MOVIE AND
   THEN GOING TO A PAY SEX SITE

Escape behaviors: _____

_____

_____

3. _____

Escape behaviors: _____

_____

_____

_____

Finally, choose three situations—one that is quite low risk, one that presents a more moderate risk, and a high-risk situation—and write the situation and your escape plan for each on an index card. Keep those three cards with you at all times. You may also find that referring to them occasionally will help remind you of your goals in recovery.

These three aphorisms also offer sound advice:

- "Forewarned is forearmed."
- "An ounce of prevention is worth a pound of cure."
- "Be prepared!"

Exercise 11: Writing a Letter to Yourself

This exercise will help you become more aware of the ways your cybersex behaviors have affected other people in your life—your partner, a close friend, work colleague, or others. Choose one of these people and, putting yourself in this person's shoes, write a letter to yourself from his or her perspective about your cybersex use and how he or she has been affected by it.

When you've finished your letter, leave it for a day or so. Then read it again.

Are you surprised by what you wrote? Explain your answer.

_____

_____

_____

_____

Had you ever before considered how this person or others might have been affected by your behavior? What feelings do you have about this now?

_____

_____

_____

_____

In what ways have others been affected by your behaviors? How does it feel to try to see your actions from another's perspective?

_____

_____

_____

_____

At the beginning of this workbook, we talked about the isolating nature of cybersex. You are not really interacting in a physical way with another human being. You're interacting with a computer and images on a TV monitor. With cybersex, it is easier than with other types of sexual-acting-out behavior to forget or ignore the fact that your behaviors are actually affecting other people. You become so immersed in the fantasy and trance it creates that you don't think about anything but yourself. But now you see that your behaviors do affect others in your life.

To Optimize Your Recovery

By now, you realize how important it is to embrace the First Order changes as described in chapter 4 and the Transition changes we've described here. First Order changes are meant to be stopgap measures. They are only surface measures. On their own, they will not help you address the causes of the problem, which are deeper and take more time to work through. They will, however, help you quickly get your life under control and set the stage for the deeper work to be done with Transition and Second Order changes. They will allow you to build a strong support system that you can rely on for the rest of your life.

Remember That Support Is Nearby—as Close as Our Internet Web Site

Remember that the Internet can provide a positive and therapeutic experience. We have developed a Web site (www.sexhelp.com) specifically to support you, the readers of this workbook. You will find that it has information and articles about problematic sexual behavior, research on what works and what doesn't work for recovery support, and a number of exercises you can do that will give you a safe and positive computer and Internet experience—one that can enhance your recovery efforts.

CHAPTER 6: *Changing the Way You Live*

Your involvement with cybersex and its effect on your life and the lives of those close to you may now be causing overwhelming feelings of fear, worry, confusion, sadness, anger, and guilt. The road to healing may seem difficult, even impossible, but don't give in to despair. There is hope!

Perhaps you have reached that quiet moment of surrender, realizing that you have a problem with cybersex and that you really do need to do something about it. Or maybe you're not yet sure about your commitment to changing your cybersex behaviors. You may be wondering whether it's really worth the trouble and the effort. Whatever stage you are at, it is important to acknowledge your feelings and move on.

Our work with thousands of people who are recovering from compulsive or addictive behavior has shown us that there are predictable stages people pass through as they descend into more and more problematic compulsive and addictive behaviors and as they recover from these behaviors. While we can't say for certain what you will experience in recovery if you follow the steps we lay out, you will be able to relate to these commonly shared experiences.

Second Order Changes—On a Path to Long-Term Change

In chapters 4 and 5, we discussed First Order changes—the concrete actions taken to quickly stop a problem and to address specific consequences. We also dicussed Transition changes—those changes that help you bridge the crisis managing steps of First Order change with Second Order changes. We will now introduce you to these Second Order changes—the steps that you take to actually change the dynamics of your life and the way you live.

Second Order changes will set you on a path to long-term recovery. While your situation may feel quite hopeless or even desperate at this moment, those who have traveled this path before you have found that over time, a completely new way of living can emerge. This new life, you will discover, will be well worth the pain and effort of the work you're in the midst of right now. Though it may be nearly impossible to imagine, you may eventually come to see this struggle as a treasured gift—one that has given you a new life that is more rich and fulfilling than you ever imagined possible.

Hermes and Hermes' Web

A special tool that we find effective in helping people understand the complex nature of compulsive and addictive behaviors—as well as the process of recovery from them—is called Hermes' Web.[1]

Who or what is Hermes? One of the Greek pantheon, Hermes is the connector, the god of the crossroads. All things meet on Hermes' ground—sexuality, business, ethics, medicine, and criminality. Hermes weaves them together. Hermes has the ability to move in and out of all other worlds freely and is never held captive. He is known for connecting high and low, living and dead, dark and light, and all manner of things.

Hermes is nonauthoritarian, an equalizer, creating symmetry and equality in relationships and politics. His aim is not power, but imagination and connection. Hermes is the friendliest of gods and works to connect the human and the divine, however estranged they may become. As the Greek god of thieves, borders, and commerce, Hermes is not afraid to combine elements, to take from here or there to put together what works rather than play by the rules and be ineffective.

Hermes seeks to keep life alive, mercurial, and vibrant. Hermes is also the desire for life, the yearning and urge to be alive, to explore, mix, and tangle. His fleetness is his excitement. He brings diversity and friendliness to the world, connecting all its elements.

This tool is called Hermes' Web to honor the interconnectedness of life, both internal and external, and to honor the One whose role it is to bring awareness and soulfulness to life. Hermes' Web allows people to visualize their internal landscape and thus facilitate Hermes' work. It is a tool that demonstrates how everything in a person is interconnected, whether conscious or unconscious. Hermes' Web also demonstrates the negative consequences of various degrees of disconnection.

Figure 6.1

HERMES' WEB

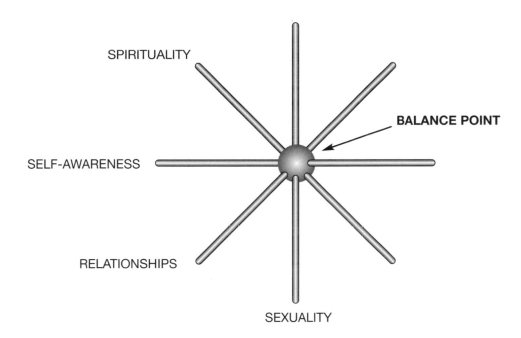

We use Hermes' Web and its representation of the human personality as a tool to illustrate some of the differences between First and Second Order changes. First Order changes are changes that take place at our ego, or personality, level. These changes are visible, distinct, and obvious. On Hermes' Web, these changes are represented by its points.

We can also use each of the four arms of Hermes' Web to represent four important areas of recovery: relationships, sexuality, spirituality, and self-awareness. The ends of each arm are that area's extremes. For example, at one endpoint on the arm of sexuality would be sexually compulsive and addictive behaviors; at the other would be the complete denial of sexuality—sexual anorexia. Can you see how you have tended to live or act at one extreme and then its opposite?

The deeper and more complex levels of Second Order changes are represented by the center of Hermes' Web, where the arms intersect one another. The center represents a balance point, and Second Order changes are designed to help you create balance in your life.

In the remainder of this chapter, we will focus on these four recovery areas. You'll learn more about the role they play in your life and in successful recovery. Exercises will also be provided to help you more easily explore these areas. You will find that working on them by yourself will be valuable, but we strongly encourage you to share them with your therapist, too. With his or her help, these exercises will provide you with a deeper understanding of this material and yourself.

[Note: You may view a picture of Hermes' Web at: www.hermesweb.com. If you would like your own Hermes' Web, please see "Hermes' Web and the Web Sight Program" in the appendix.]

Relationships

People who use cybersex compulsively or addictively often find themselves at an extreme of the relationship continuum: isolated from most of the people in their lives. Others at this extreme are those who generally withdraw—who perhaps have limited social skills, are socially inept, and who have great difficulty forming meaningful relationships.

At the other end of this arm of Hermes' Web are people who have few, if any, boundaries with regard to their relationships. People in this category may think they are "friends" with everyone; they have little respect for others' personal boundaries and generally take little care in choosing the people in their lives.

We have relationships with others in a number of different categories—with our children, parents, siblings, and our extended family; people with whom we grew up; and various friends, acquaintences, and work colleagues. We have romantic relationships and relationships with sponsors and with professionals such as our family doctor, therapist, and tax accountant.

With so many people in our lives, how do we find a balance? Not everyone can be a "best friend." We share different parts of ourselves with the many people in our lives. It's important to be able to discern those with whom we are safe—those who will keep our trust and confidences. To maintain balance in this part of our lives, we don't want to become too isolated, nor can we overextend ourselves by trying to be everything to everyone.

The three relationship-related exercises that follow will help you learn more about your relationships and finding a relationship balance that is appropriate for you.

Exercise 1: Family Dynamics

This exercise will help you explore the dynamics of the relationships in the family in which you grew up. To do this exercise properly, you will need to think of your family as a system. By this we mean the ways your family members interacted with one another to create a whole.

Begin by drawing a large circle on a piece of paper. In the circle, write the names of all your family members, both immediate and extended, who took part in and influenced the life of your family.

Then, think about all these people. Here are some questions you can ask yourself to better understand how your family's members interacted and the kind of people they were. These questions are meant to get you started. You'll find many more relationship connections and roles in your family system as you work through this exercise.

- Who was a leader in your family?
- Who did what tasks?
- When there were problems, who helped solve them?
- Were there alliances among family members? With whom?
- Were some family members closer to Dad or to Mom?

- Did Dad and Mom work as a team?

- If only one parent was active in the family, did someone else (a family friend, grandparent, or other person) help with day-to-day family life?

- To whom did you turn to get your way?

- Who helped you when you needed help?

- Was anyone abused in your family? Who?

- What kinds of addictions run in your family?

- Were you close to one or both parents?

- What "roles" did you and other family members play? Examples of common roles include caretaker, troublemaker, peacemaker, enforcer, goody two-shoes, princess, court jester, and recluse.

Answering questions like these will help you begin to see your family as a system.

Now you are ready to add this information to your drawing. Maybe you'll draw a wall between you and your dad because you weren't close to him, but a circle around your name and your mom because the two of you stuck closely together. Perhaps you will draw a tavern outside the circle and draw a circle around your dad and the tavern to show where his priorities were. You might draw another circle around yourself and a sister as a symbol of the alliance you had with her. You could draw an arrow between yourself and a brother to show conflict.

As you begin indicating these dynamics, ask yourself what purpose these dynamics served in the family. How did the family "system" work?

Once you have created this diagram, you might want to do another to help you understand the workings of your mother's and father's families. If you're married or in a partner relationship, examine it using this method.

This exercise can help you understand much about how you grew up and how you became the person you are today. It will also help you discover traits that you may have learned as a child and are still unconsciously carrying with you into your current relationships.

How, for example, did your parents' family systems provide a model for the one you grew up in?

_____

_____

_____

_____

Do you retain and carry out the role you took on from your family in your current relationships? If so, explain.

_____

_____

_____

_____

_____

When you are done, show your work to your therapist and to others in your support group for further discussion.

Exercise 2: Looking at Your Friendships

At the beginning of this section on relationships, we talked about the need to strike a balance when choosing and building friendships with so many people in our lives. As we said, not everyone can be a "best friend." This exercise will help you look at your friendships and determine whether your relationships are in or out of balance.

At the right you will see three circles in the form of a bull's-eye. Before you begin, think of the people in your life (excluding your immediate family members). You might even make a list of them in the outside margin of the page.

Place these people into one of three categories:

1. Close, intimate friends: These are people you trust implicitly and with whom you can, and do, share everything, even your deepest feelings and concerns and embarrassing moments. You would trust these people with any problem. A person with whom you are romantically involved might be in this group, but perhaps not. Write the names of these people in the center circle.

2. Acquaintances: You are not as close to the people in this group. Those in this group could include business colleagues, people with whom you play sports, neighbors, your car mechanic, your hair stylist, a neighbor you regularly have coffee with, a jogging or golf buddy, or members of your book club. These are people you might not trust with your deepest secrets, but they are people you enjoy being around. You don't know everything about one another, but you still have a nice connection. Some of these people might, with effort and desire on your part, become part of your group of closest friends. Write the names of these people in the second circle.

3. Negative influences: These are people in your life who do not offer you a healthy relationship. They might be fun to hang with, entertaining, and energetic, but when you are with them, your activities are not healthy and good for you. This might be a person who likes to frequent strip clubs or visits porn sites. It might be a woman who likes to go to bars just to hustle guys or who spends hours in sexually oriented chat rooms. It might be a person who has few, if any, close friends and whose attempts at intimate relationships continue to fail. These are people whose influence tends to lead you away from the better parts of yourself. Write the names of these people in the outer circle.

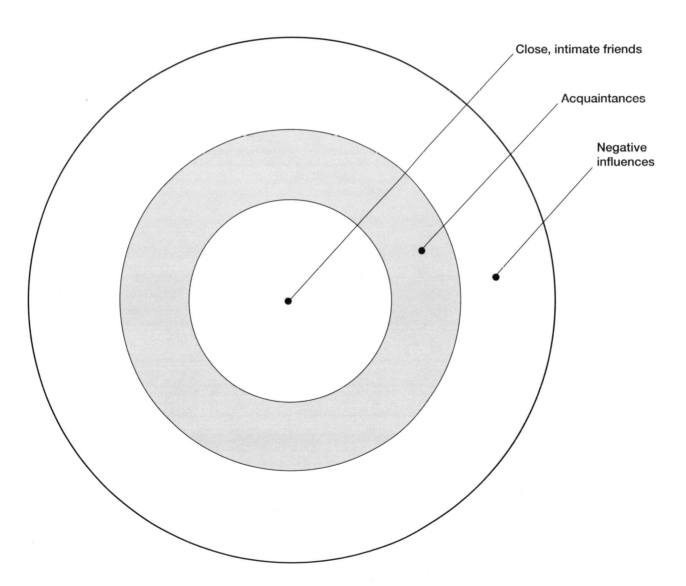

Close, intimate friends

Acquaintances

Negative influences

When you have finished placing people within these three circles, look closely at what you have done and think about what this means. Don't worry if some circles have more names than others or even if a circle has no names. Place the names only where you truly think each belongs.

Do you have any people in the center circle? If there's no one, or only one or two people, this indicates that you currently have difficulty sharing who you really are with others. It also suggests that you'll need to find a way to add to this group to get the support you'll need for recovering from your cybersex behaviors. A core group of close friends in your life can help you in many ways, in addition to helping you with your work in recovery.

A large number of people in the center circle with few in the middle one might indicate that your personal boundaries are too loose. You let just about anyone into your "inner circle."

Look at your outer circle. A larger number of names there might suggest that you have many people in your life whose influence will not help your efforts to recover from your cybersex behaviors.

Your goal is relationship balance: having a few close people in your inner circle and a larger group of kind and supportive people in the middle circle, with few, if any, in the outer circle.

When people first start recovery, often they don't have good boundaries. As a result, they try to bring all the people in their lives into their inner circle. Such people might, for example, want to tell their boss their whole cybersex story, even though this isn't an appropriate relationship in which to do this. When recovery challenges arise, some people turn to their outer-circle friends—usually a very unwise decision.

In the space below, write what you notice about your particular relationship balance. If you have questions about what you've done here, write them down, too, and discuss them with your therapist, sponsor, or support group.

_____

_____

_____

_____

_____

_____

_____

_____

Sexuality

Another arm of the Hermes' Web is sexuality. At one end of the sexual spectrum are people who are sexually anorexic—a state in which the physical, mental, and emotional task of avoiding sex dominates one's life. "Sexual anorexia" does not mean inhibited sexual desire or sexual dysfunction. Sexual anorexics are consumed by a dread of sexual pleasure and filled with fear and sexual self-doubt. At the opposite end of this arm are people who are sexually compulsive and addictive—those whose sexual behaviors are out of control.

This workbook's goal is to help you begin to see sex as an authentic expression of self that can be safe and loving. A parallel exists between sexual compulsivity and compulsive eating. Compulsive overeaters do not give up food; they learn how to eat differently. They learn about their emotional relationship to food and how they have misused food. They learn to choose different kinds of foods based on a food plan that identifies what is healthy for them.

While thousands of articles and hundreds of books talk about sexual dysfunction, professionals have seldom focused on the components of healthy sexuality. Few have come forward to say what healthy sexuality looks like.

In his groundbreaking book *Sexual Anorexia: Overcoming Sexual Self-Hatred*,[2] Patrick Carnes presents a superb program for exploring your sexuality. It is composed of twelve dimensions of sexual experiences. These dimensions represent principles he describes as the basic elements of healthy sexuality: mutuality and equality, individual respect and dignity, and commitment to nonabusive, nonviolent, and nonexploitive loving relationships that add meaning to life.

The following exercise is based on these dimensions. It will help you explore these dimensions in your life and see how your cybersex behaviors affect them.

In *Sexual Anorexia*, Dr. Carnes presents a more in-depth program for exploring the twelve dimensions of human sexuality. He devotes a chapter of this book to each dimension, and at the end of each are activities designed to help foster and develop that specific dimension of healthy sexuality in one's life. These activities can also easily be used with a partner. We are certain that you will find this work valuable in your recovery.

Exercise 3: Healthy Sexuality

PART A

The twelve dimensions of healthy sexuality are listed below. After each are questions that will help you begin to explore these dimensions in your life and learn how your cybersex behaviors affect them. When you have finished this exercise, you will have a much better idea of the areas you need to work with in order to have a more healthy sexuality. Sharing this exercise and its results with your therapist will help you gain even more benefit from your work here.

1. Nurturing: The capacity to receive care from others and provide care for self.

Describe the state of this dimension in your life. Are you doing well here? Explain your answer.

_____

_____

_____

_____

Are you satisfied with your understanding of this dimension? If not, what don't you understand about it?

_____

_____

_____

_____

Are you comfortable with your ability to express the qualities described in this dimension, or do you feel you need more work in this area? Please explain.

_____

_____

_____

_____

How would you choose to change in respect to this dimension? Why?

_____

_____

_____

_____

How have your cybersex behaviors affected you in this dimension?

_____

_____

_____

_____

2. Sensuality: The mindfulness of physical senses that creates emotional, intellectual, spiritual, and physical presence.

Describe the state of this dimension in your life. Are you doing well here? Explain your answer.

_____

_____

_____

_____

Are you satisfied with your understanding of this dimension? If not, what don't you understand about it?

_____

_____

_____

_____

Are you comfortable with your ability to express the qualities described in this dimension, or do you feel you need more work in this area? Please explain.

_____

_____

_____

_____

How would you choose to change in respect to this dimension? Why?

_____

_____

_____

How have your cybersex behaviors affected you in this dimension?

_____

_____

_____

_____

3. Self-image: A positive self-perception that includes embracing your sexual self.

Describe the state of this dimension in your life. Are you doing well here? Explain your answer.

_____

_____

_____

_____

Are you satisfied with your understanding of this dimension? If not, what don't you understand about it?

_____

_____

_____

_____

Are you comfortable with your ability to express the qualities described in this dimension, or do you feel you need more work in this area? Please explain.

_____

_____

_____

_____

How would you choose to change in respect to this dimension? Why?

_____

_____

_____

_____

How have your cybersex behaviors affected you in this dimension?

_____

_____

_____

_____

4. Self-definition: A clear knowledge of who you are as a person, both positive and negative, and the ability to express boundaries as well as needs.

Describe the state of this dimension in your life. Are you doing well here? Explain your answer.

_____

_____

_____

_____

Are you satisfied with your understanding of this dimension? If not, what don't you understand about it?

_____

_____

_____

_____

Are you comfortable with your ability to express the qualities described in this dimension, or do you feel you need more work in this area? Please explain.

_____

_____

_____

_____

How would you choose to change in respect to this dimension? Why?

_____

_____

_____

_____

How have your cybersex behaviors affected you in this dimension?

_____

_____

_____

_____

5. Comfort: The capacity to be at ease about sexual matters with oneself and with others.

Describe the state of this dimension in your life. Are you doing well here? Explain your answer.

_____

_____

_____

_____

Are you satisfied with your understanding of this dimension? If not, what don't you understand about it?

_____

_____

_____

_____

Are you comfortable with your ability to express the qualities described in this dimension, or do you feel you need more work in this area? Please explain.

_____

_____

_____

_____

How would you choose to change in respect to this dimension? Why?

_____

_____

_____

_____

How have your cybersex behaviors affected you in this dimension?

_____

_____

_____

_____

6. Knowledge: The knowledge base about sex in general and about one's own unique sexual patterns.

Describe the state of this dimension in your life. Are you doing well here? Explain your answer.

_____

_____

_____

_____

Are you satisfied with your understanding of this dimension? If not, what don't you understand about it?

_____

_____

_____

_____

Are you comfortable with your ability to express the qualities described in this dimension, or do you feel you need more work in this area? Please explain.

_____

_____

_____

_____

How would you choose to change in respect to this dimension? Why?

_____

_____

_____

_____

How have your cybersex behaviors affected you in this dimension?

_____

_____

_____

_____

7. Relationship: A capacity to have intimacy and friendship with those of the same and the opposite gender.

Describe the state of this dimension in your life. Are you doing well here? Explain your answer.

_____

_____

_____

_____

Are you satisfied with your understanding of this dimension? If not, what don't you understand about it?

_____

_____

_____

_____

Are you comfortable with your ability to express the qualities described in this dimension, or do you feel you need more work in this area? Please explain.

_____

_____

_____

_____

How would you choose to change in respect to this dimension? Why?

_____

_____

_____

_____

How have your cybersex behaviors affected you in this dimension?

_____

_____

_____

_____

8. Partnership: The ability to maintain an interdependent, equal relationship that is intimate and erotic.

Describe the state of this dimension in your life. Are you doing well here? Explain your answer

_____

_____

_____

_____

Are you satisfied with your understanding of this dimension? If not, what don't you understand about it?

_____

_____

_____

_____

Are you comfortable with your ability to express the qualities described in this dimension, or do you feel you need more work in this area? Please explain.

_____

_____

_____

_____

How would you choose to change in respect to this dimension? Why?

_____

_____

_____

_____

How have your cybersex behaviors affected you in this dimension?

_____

_____

_____

_____

9. Nongenital sex: The ability to express erotic desire emotionally and physically without the use of the genitals.

Describe the state of this dimension in your life. Are you doing well here? Explain your answer.

_____

_____

_____

_____

Are you satisfied with your understanding of this dimension? If not, what don't you understand about it?

_____

_____

_____

_____

Are you comfortable with your ability to express the qualities described in this dimension, or do you feel you need more work in this area? Please explain.

_____

_____

_____

_____

How would you choose to change in respect to this dimension? Why?

_____

_____

_____

_____

How have your cybersex behaviors affected you in this dimension?

_____

_____

_____

_____

10. Genital sex: The ability to freely express erotic feelings with the use of the genitals.

Describe the state of this dimension in your life. Are you doing well here? Explain your answer.

_____

_____

_____

_____

Are you satisfied with your understanding of this dimension? If not, what don't you understand about it?

_____

_____

_____

_____

Are you comfortable with your ability to express the qualities described in this dimension, or do you feel you need more work in this area? Please explain.

_____

_____

_____

_____

How would you choose to change in respect to this dimension? Why?

_____

_____

_____

_____

How have your cybersex behaviors affected you in this dimension?

_____

_____

_____

_____

11. Spirituality: The ability to connect sexual desire and expression to the value and meaning of one's life.

Describe the state of this dimension in your life. Are you doing well here? Explain your answer.

_____

_____

_____

_____

Are you satisfied with your understanding of this dimension? If not, what don't you understand about it?

_____

_____

_____

_____

Are you comfortable with your ability to express the qualities described in this dimension, or do you feel you need more work in this area? Please explain.

_____

_____

_____

_____

How would you choose to change in respect to this dimension? Why?

_____

_____

_____

_____

How have your cybersex behaviors affected you in this dimension?

_____

_____

_____

_____

12. Passion: The capacity to express deeply held feelings of desire and meaning about one's sexual self, relationships, and intimacy experience.

Describe the state of this dimension in your life. Are you doing well here? Explain your answer.

_____

_____

_____

_____

Are you satisfied with your understanding of this dimension? If not, what don't you understand about it?

_____

_____

_____

Are you comfortable with your ability to express the qualities described in this dimension, or do you feel you need more work in this area? Please explain.

_____

_____

_____

How would you choose to change in respect to this dimension? Why?

_____

_____

_____

How have your cybersex behaviors affected you in this dimension?

_____

_____

_____

PART B

Take a moment to look back on times you have been sexual. How have you come to the decision to be sexual with someone or with yourself? Did you think about it at all, or did you tend to just follow your feelings and desires?

Ask yourself the following twelve questions about being sexual. Your answers will help you better see your motivations for sex. They will also help you thoughtfully decide whether sex in a given situation will be a healthy or an unhealthy action.

1. Do I feel hopeless, angry, hurt, lonely, or sad?   Yes ☐   No ☐

2. Would this act be loving toward me (and my partner)?   Yes ☐   No ☐

3. Have I looked through my program of First, Transition, and Second Order changes lately?
    Am I getting fuzzy about my boundaries and about what defines a slip for me?   Yes ☐   No ☐

4. Do I feel reasonably centered? Do I feel connected to my Higher Power?   Yes ☐   No ☐

5. Do I feel sexual, or am I choosing to be sexual just to please someone else?   Yes ☐   No ☐

6. Have I been having obsessive thoughts about being sexual today? Has a major sexual trigger
    hit me today—one that is impairing my thinking?   Yes ☐   No ☐

7. Where am I? Is this a healthy environment for me to be sexual in?   Yes ☐   No ☐

8. Is what I am thinking of doing within my values?   Yes ☐   No ☐

9. Am I choosing to be sexual just because I feel physically ill, because I have time on my hands, or
    because I am dreading being alone?   Yes ☐   No ☐

10. If I choose to be sexual, will I fantasize?   Would fantasy distance me from my Higher Power?
    Yes ☐   No ☐

11. Does my desire to have sex at this time feel too powerful?   Yes ☐   No ☐

12. Will I most likely have strong feelings of shame if I go ahead with being sexual in this way?
    Yes ☐   No ☐

Spirituality

Our spirituality, represented by the third arm on Hermes's Web, is the expression of our search for meaning in life. How did we come to be born? How is it that we are conscious of ourselves? What is the purpose of life? What is the purpose of my life? What is the right way to live? Is there a power greater than myself, and if so, does it play a role in my life? How we answer these fundamental questions gives direction to our lives.

While many people turn to organized religions for answers, religion and spirituality are not necessarily synonymous. One can be very spiritual and have nothing to do with religion and, conversely, a person who participates faithfully in religious practices may have no sense of a deeper spirituality.

Is there a connection between spirituality and sexuality? Yes, but unfortunately, we often see the relationship between sexuality and spirituality as a war in which one must defeat and destroy the other. This struggle is a futile one. Our sexuality arises out of a sense of incompleteness that is manifested by the desire to unite through the sexual act in order to once again be united with the Divine.

This is not myth; it's human experience. In *The Road Less Traveled*, M. Scott Peck writes, "When my beloved first stands before me naked, all open to my sight, there is a feeling throughout the whole of me. Awe! Why Awe? If sex is no more than an instinct, why don't I simply feel horny or hungry? Such simple hunger would be quite sufficient to ensure the propagation of the species. Why should sex be complicated with reverence?"

Sex is "complicated with reverence" because it is, in fact, the closest many people ever come to a mystical experience. Indeed, this is why so many people chase after sex with such desperate abandon. Whether or not they know it, they are searching for God.

Abraham Maslow, in his studies of self-actualizing people, discovered that they often experience orgasm as a religious, even mystical event. Maslow made it clear that these people were not speaking metaphorically. With another human in deeply loving relationships, we can touch the Divine through sex. Ironically, however, though we need the other to reach these heights, we briefly lose that other at the climactic moment, forgetting who and where we are. Mystics and spiritual teachers through the ages have spoken of the necessity of an "ego death" as a necessary part of the spiritual journey—even its goal, and the French refer to orgasm as the "little death." We have entered the realm of spirit. Sex and spirit become one as we become one with All.

The common denominator of sex and spirituality is the search for meaning. Sexuality and spirituality connect through meaning. As we deepen our understanding of ourselves, of others, of our planet and all its myriad life, we heighten both our spirituality and our sexuality. As Peck is fond of saying, "I distrust any religious conversion which does not also involve an intensification of one's sexuality." The deeper and more meaningful our sexuality, the more we touch the mystical.

We need to recognize that we are part of a much larger whole, and it's when people are unable to make this connection that they turn to relationships with objects—the false gods, in the biblical sense, of alcohol, money, sex (and cybersex), food—whatever seems to fill the void inside. While still a search for meaning, this path leads to addiction and a life that is unmanageable and out of control.

At one end of the Hermes' Web arm of spirituality are people who have little interest in the spiritual quest and seldom, if ever, acknowledge that a spiritual force might be at work in their lives. At the other are people whose spiritual quest is expressed in rigid religions and religious practices. Once again, your goal is to find a balance in this area of your life .

Learning more about these timeless and puzzling questions can take many forms. Organized religions are one of the most common places people turn, and many find this very helpful. Other people may use Eastern spiritual practices such as yoga and meditation. Still others turn to nature and find profound comfort in the outdoors. Support groups, therapy, and Twelve Step groups have also helped countless people in their spiritual journey. Furthermore, none of these choices is mutually exclusive. Many people incorporate two or more in their lives.

Exercise 4: Exploring Spirituality

What did you learn about religion/spirituality, if anything, as a child?

_____

_____

_____

_____

Is spirituality a part of your life today? If not, why not? If it is, explain in what ways.

_____

_____

_____

_____

What does spirituality mean to you?

_____

_____

_____

_____

Do you incorporate spiritual practices in your life? Explain.

_____

_____

_____

_____

How do these practices affect and influence your life?

_____

_____

_____

_____

What benefit do you feel you receive from your spiritual practices?

_____

_____

_____

_____

Do you want to explore this part of your life more in the future? If so, why?

_____

_____

_____

_____

How would you do this?

_____

_____

_____

_____

Do you see your work in recovering from cybersex behaviors as being related to your spirituality? Explain.

_____

_____

_____

_____

Self-Awareness

Self-awareness, represented by the fourth arm on Hermes's Web, means exactly that—to be aware of yourself as an entity and personality, to be aware of your feelings, needs, motivations, goals, and so forth. Self-awareness involves both intellectual and emotional intelligence. The concept of "emotional intelligence" is brilliantly explored in Daniel Goleman's fascinating book *Emotional Intelligence: Why It Can Matter More Than IQ.*[3] The following discussion on this topic draws from Goleman's work.

In recent years, says Goleman, a growing group of psychologists has come to agree that the old concepts of intellience quotient (IQ) revolved around a narrow band of linguistic and math skills, and that doing well on IQ tests was most directly a predictor of success in the classroom or as a professor, but less and less so as life's paths diverged from academe. These psychologists have taken a wider view of intelligence, trying to reinvent it in terms of what it takes to lead life successfully. And the result of that work has led to a growing appreciation of just how crucial "personal," or emotional, intelligence is.

We can look at emotional intelligence (EQ) in terms of five main ability areas as described below:

1. Knowing one's emotions. Self-awareness—recognizing a feeling *as it happens*—is the keystone of emotional intelligence. The ability to monitor feelings—guilt, grief, anxiety, fear, shame, joy, and so on—from moment to moment is crucial to psychological insight and self-understanding. An inability to notice our true feelings leaves us at their mercy. People with greater certainty about their feelings are better pilots of their lives, having a surer sense of how they really feel about personal decisions, from whom to marry to what job to take.

2. Managing emotions. Handling feelings so they are appropriate is an ability that builds on self-awareness. This is the capacity to soothe oneself, to shake off rampant anxiety, gloom, or irritability—and the consequences of failure at this basic emotional skill. People who are poor in this ability are constantly battling feelings of distress, while those who excel in it can bounce back far more quickly from life's setbacks and upsets.

3. Motivating oneself. Marshaling emotions in the service of a goal is essential for paying attention, for self-motivation and mastery, and for creativity. Emotional self-control—delaying gratification and stifling impulsiveness—underlies accomplishment of every sort. And being able to get into the "flow" state enables outstanding performance of all kinds. People who have this skill tend to be more highly productive and effective in whatever they undertake.

4. Recognizing emotions of others. Empathy, another ability that builds on emotional self-awareness, is the fundamental "people skill." People who are empathic are more attuned to the subtle social signals that indicate what others need or want. This makes them better at callings such as the caring professions, teaching, sales, and management.

5. Handling relationships. The art of handling relationships is, in large part, skill in managing emotions in others. These are the abilities that support popularity, leadership, and interpersonal effectiveness. People who excel in these skills do well at anything that relies on interacting smoothly with others; they are social stars.

Clearly, people differ in their abilities in each of these domains. Some of us may be quite adept, for example, at handling our own anxiety but relatively inept at soothing someone else's upsets. Emotional skills can be improved; to a great extent, each of these domains represents a group of habits and responses that, with the right effort, can be changed.

IQ and emotional intelligence are not opposing competencies, but rather separate ones. We all mix intellect and emotional acuity: people with a high IQ but low emotional intelligence (or low IQ and high emotional intelligence) are, despite the stereotypes, relatively rare.

At one end of the self-awareness arm of the Hermes' Web is a relative lack of awareness of one's self. These people have little insight about how their behavior is affected by the way they feel. On the other end are people who have a false sense of self-awareness—"faux-awareness." They are narcissistic and egotistical, self-important, and generally lack any humility whatsoever.

For clear examples of emotional intelligence, or lack thereof, we can turn to the arenas of professional athletics and the music/acting business. Wonderfully talented athletes, musicians, and actors often exhibit a startling lack of emotional intelligence. Think of NBA player Latrell Sprewell, who forfeited a $24 million contract for striking and threatening to kill his coach in a fit of anger. Christian Slater, Robert Downey Jr., and Marilyn Monroe were all very intelligent and talented performers whose lives unraveled because they didn't have the emotional intelligence to handle the pressure and demands that came with their success. Emotional intelligence is like a good manager who handles a performer's business while he or she focuses on talent. Without emotional intelligence, you can waste your talents, squander your energy, and abuse your charm and personal influence. Emotional intelligence is the ability to function and excel under pressure, not just when the going is easy and no obstacles lie in your path. It means having depth and character.

You use your emotional intelligence to keep your life in balance—to keep yourself living in the center of Hermes' Web. Often people believe their problems with cybersex are related to how smart they are. From the outside, we can look at people who have gotten into trouble for their sexual behavior, and say, "How could they have done that? Any idiot would have known that they were going to get caught!" Such a statement assumes that the problem is the result of stupidity. It isn't. It stems from a lack of emotional intelligence. Many very bright people struggle with compulsive and addictive cybersex behaviors. Unless you work to develop your emotional intelligence, staying in recovery will be difficult.

While the following exercises each have a different focus, all have the common thread of helping you become more aware of your emotional intelligence and assisting you in developing it further.

Exercise 5: Looking at Your EQ

Review the explanations of the five EQ ability areas. Next, think about your EQ abilities in each area. In the spaces below, take a few minutes to describe how you see your EQ skills in each ability area. Where are your strengths? In what areas would you like to improve?

1. Knowing one's emotions. Recognizing a feeling as it *happens* is the keystone of emotional intelligence.

_____

_____

_____

_____

2. Managing emotions. Handling feelings so they are appropriate; the capacity to soothe oneself, to shake off rampant anxiety, gloom, or irritability.

_____

_____

_____

_____

3. Motivating oneself. Emotional self-control essential for paying attention, for self-motivation and mastery, and for creativity.

_____

_____

_____

4. Recognizing emotions of others. Empathy—*the* fundamental "people skill."

_____

_____

_____

_____

5. Handling relationships. The art of relationships is, in large part, skill in managing emotions in others.

_____

_____

_____

_____

Managing Your Shame

The following exercise is intended to help you distinguish between two different and uncomfortable feelings: shame and guilt. If you are like most of us, you have probably used these words interchangeably in the past. Shame and guilt are not the same, however, and in this exercise, you will learn how they are different and why it is so important to be able to recognize this difference. You'll also see why guilt is a healthy feeling and why shame is not useful and interferes with your emotional intelligence abilities.

As we use the word "guilt," it stands for uncomfortable feelings you may have about something you have done (or have neglected to do). For instance, you may have guilty feelings about not getting to work on time or for not doing a task you'd promised your child you'd do. Guilt has to do with your actions. "Shame," on the other hand, is a negative feeling you have about yourself as a person. Feeling stupid and worthless are shameful feelings.

Feelings of guilt and shame are often connected, which can make the process of separating them confusing. For example, let's say that you are late for work and your boss comments on the fact that you have been late several times in the last month. You may already be feeling bad about being late on this occasion, which has to do with your action today (guilt). But you may also begin to think about how you can't seem to do anything right or that you are a loser. You may see this one action as a reflection of the kind of person you are—and this is shame.

It is important to learn to recognize the difference between guilt and shame because guilt is often healthy, while shame rarely is. Guilt is healthy because it helps motivate us to change behaviors that get us into trouble or hurt other people. For example, you would probably not have done anything about your cybersex behavior if you didn't have some guilty feelings about it.

Shame, however, is a kind of self-abuse. It sends us negative messages about ourselves that undermine our self-esteem. In addition, these messages are either partly or entirely untrue. Just because you were late for work, for example, doesn't mean you're a bad or worthless person.

In this exercise, your task will be to learn to identify when you are feeling guilt and when you are feeling shame—and then to act positively on the guilt feelings and learn to avoid shame.

The key to distinguishing between shame and guilt is paying attention to what you are telling yourself. When you tell yourself you did something wrong, that is guilt. When you tell yourself something is wrong with you as a person, that is shame.

Exercise 6: The Difference between Guilt and Shame

For this assignment, identify ten self-statements that lead to guilty feelings and ten self-statements that lead to shameful feelings.

GUILT STATEMENTS (ACTION)	SHAME STATEMENTS (SELF-ATTACKS)
Example: I forgot to pay a bill.	**I am stupid and can't do anything right.**
1. _____	1. _____
_____	_____
2. _____	2. _____
_____	_____
3. _____	3. _____
_____	_____

GUILT STATEMENTS (ACTION)	SHAME STATEMENTS (SELF-ATTACKS)
4. _____	4. _____
5. _____	5. _____
6. _____	6. _____
7. _____	7. _____
8. _____	8. _____
9. _____	9. _____
10. _____	10. _____

Exercise 7: Controlling and Countering Feelings of Shame

The form on page 202 will help you rethink and analyze your shaming statements and should give you greater ability to interrupt and control them, thus helping you reduce shame's effect on you.

First, choose several of the shaming statements you have identified that most affect you. Write your first one in the "Shaming Statement" column.

The next column asks you to think about where you first experienced that statement. Often, shaming statements are first learned in childhood from people we respect, such as parents, teachers, or siblings. Sometimes, we are told shaming statements directly (for instance, "You are so stupid!"). Other shaming statements are implied silently—a disapproving look, for instance. Try to remember the earliest times you heard shaming statements and write the names of those people who gave them to you in this second column. Think about these people. When we are young children, we believe that grown-ups know a lot and that they wouldn't tell us anything that wasn't true. Now that we are adults, we know differently. We know that adults make mistakes and say things that are hurtful and untrue, even to their children and to students they teach. With this knowledge, you can begin to rethink the accuracy of these shaming statements. Are they true now? Were they ever true? What is wrong, for example with the shaming statement "I'm a loser"?

In the third column, write what is wrong with the shaming statements you have chosen.

In the final column, write your "proofs" that the shaming statements you chose are not true. To prove that you are not a "loser," give examples of things you have done correctly and well in your life. These examples don't have to be particularly grand; they need only be actions that a "loser" could not accomplish. The more specific your examples, the better.

After you have filled in the columns, you can use the information you have gathered to counter these shaming statements the next time you notice that you are saying them in your head. Here is an example:

"Man, I'm a loser."

That's not true. My father told me that when he was angry and drinking. He said that to put me down, not because it was true. It's not true now, either. I graduated from high school. I've got a steady job, and I just got a good pay raise two months ago because I'm doing a good job. My wife and kids care about me, and I'm working hard in my treatment to deal with the problems I do have. If I was really a loser, I couldn't and wouldn't have accomplished all this.

Countering shame messages once or twice probably won't eliminate them from your thinking. You'll need to be patient and consistent in taking them on. After all, they didn't get into your thinking overnight, and they won't disappear overnight, either. Remember, however, that you can control your shaming statements and eventually hear them less and less.

SHAMING STATEMENT	PERSON WHO SAID THIS	SHAMING STATEMENT ERRORS	PROOFS
1.			
2.			
3.			
4.			

Exercise 8: The "Ripple Effect" of Your Cybersex Behaviors

As we've seen, emotional intelligence has much to do with recognizing the emotions of others. When people become immersed in cybersex, they lose their ability to empathize with others.

Your cybersex behaviors have had an effect that can be likened to that of throwing a pebble into a lake. Like the ripples that move out from the point where the pebble enters the water, the effects of your cybersex behaviors have rippled out from you to the other people in your life.

In doing this exercise, you will learn more about whom your behavior affected and in what ways it did so. In part 2, you will begin the process of making amends to those who have been hurt by your behaviors.

PART 1

Make a list of the people who have been affected by your cybersex behaviors. Write a short sentence describing how each person has been affected and/or the consequences of that behavior. People affected might include your spouse or partner, children, friends, work colleagues, school friends, or neighbors. Your place of employment (lost income because of lost productivity due to your on-the-job cybersex activities) may also have been affected. Use additional paper if you need more room. For the time being, ignore the lines labeled "How I will make amends."

Person/environment affected: _____

How affected: _____

_____

Consequence of your behavior: _____

_____

_____

How I will make amends: _____

_____

_____

_____

Person/environment affected: _____

How affected: _____

_____

Consequence of your behavior: _____

_____

_____

How I will make amends: _____

_____

_____

_____

Person/environment affected: _____

How affected: _____

_____

Consequence of your behavior: _____

_____

_____

How I will make amends: _____

_____

_____

_____

Person/environment affected: _____

How affected: _____

_____

Consequence of your behavior: _____

_____

_____

How I will make amends: _____

_____

_____

_____

Person/environment affected: _____

How affected: _____

_____

Consequence of your behavior: _____

_____

_____

How I will make amends: _____

_____

_____

_____

PART 2

Now it is time to think about how you might make amends to the people/environments affected by your cybersex behavior. You may choose to make amends directly in person, or you may choose to write a letter of amends, which you will NOT send. In some cases, it is not appropriate to contact someone who has been injured by your cybersex activities, or it may simply not be possible. In these instances, you should write a letter of amends (see below). We strongly caution you against making any amends in person without first getting advice and counsel from your sponsor or therapist. Either one can and should help you decide which people it is appropriate to make amends to in person and how to do so.]

In the "How I will make amends" space, indicate how you plan to make amends to each person on your list .

Exercise 9: Sample Letter of Amends

If you write a letter of amends to someone affected by your cybersex behaviors, do not send it. The information below can serve as a guide to help you begin this effort. Incorporate this information and anything else you would like to say into your letter.

1. Tell what you did.

2. Explain how you are responsible for what you did.

3. Explain how your behavior was in no way anyone else's fault.

4. State that you accept responsibility for any feelings they have that may include betrayal, hurt, anxiety, fear, loss, confusion, guilt, shame, disgust, sadness, and so forth.

5. State that you take responsibility for any other changes they may have endured as a result of your acting out with cybersex.

If your cybersex activities involved minors, be sure to do the following in your letter:

6. Accept responsibility for utilizing the adult role to make sexual contact.

7. Accept responsibility for using the minor's sensuous feeling for sexual entrapment.

8. Accept responsibility for the distortion of the adult-child relationship.

Keeping a Journal or Diary

Emotional intelligence includes knowing and managing one's emotions and motivating oneself. Keeping a journal and practicing relaxation and mindfulness techniques can help you enhance your EQ abilities in these areas.

Keeping a log or journal that includes your sexual experiences, thoughts, feelings, and fantasies can be a big help to you as you try to sort out feelings and thoughts. In addition, it will allow you to clearly see your growth and change. Journaling is also a useful technique for exploring ideas and trying to understand your thinking process. Writing about yourself gives you the opportunity to see yourself from a different point of view and to do some self-observation without criticism. You will find that the experience of writing down your thoughts and feelings will give you a different perspective on who you are as a person. It is an opportunity for you to see your thoughts and feelings in black and white. In other words, it's a wonderful way to expand your self-awareness.

Journaling is used regularly as a homework assignment, and often assignments are given every week in group. A journal can be used not only for these assignments, but also to keep track of events and thoughts and feelings that occur during the day. It is important for you to feel that your journal is private—that it is for you to read and not anyone else. You may choose to share your journal with someone, but that is your choice. It is important that you feel that your journal is safe.

You can keep a journal in any manner that's convenient for you—in a small notebook, on a dated calendar, in a loose-leaf folder, or in a blank book designed for journaling.

How often should you write? It's up to you. You can write some thoughts or feelings and experiences every day, or you may prefer to simply jot a few lines at the end of each week, recalling highlights and reviewing homework progress. While how often you contribute to your journal is up to you, it is important to write on a regular basis. Writing regularly is helpful because it makes it easier to keep track of thoughts, feelings, and fantasies that you report on during group check-in. If you journal regularly, it will be easier for you to remember the details of the week.

Here are some tips for beginning your journal:

- Write spontaneous thoughts and feelings.
- Write everything that comes to mind.
- Allow yourself the freedom to not edit or criticize your writing.
- You need not worry about writing complete sentences or using proper grammar.

Here are some sample journal entries:

"When I got home from work, I found I had some time before dinner, so instead of reading the paper, I took the opportunity to do my relaxation exercise. It was amazing how I was able to let go of the tensions and frustrations that built up during the day. I found I enjoyed dinner a lot more after doing them."

"On my way to work this morning, I found myself thinking about my girlfriend and the last time we made love. We were both in the bedroom."

"In the middle of the afternoon, just after meeting with my boss, I was amazed to find myself thinking about the young boy across the street."

"Right now I'm feeling . . ."

"Right now I'm sitting in a chair . . ."

Breathing, Relaxation, and Mindfulness

You may have come across the term "mindfulness" and wondered what it meant. At its core, mindfulness is the state of being aware of and fully appreciating what you're thinking, feeling, and doing at any given waking moment. It's a way of perceiving life that you can achieve through diligent practice. Applied properly, mindfulness practice can be a powerful tool for personal growth, self-awareness, and self-understanding.

It will enable you to…

- Slow down, relax, and become more aware of the present.
- Realize that no thought or feeling is fixed and permanent.
- Recognize your obsessive, compulsive, defensive patterns of behavior, and the underlying, ordinarily unconscious feelings that fuel such patterns.
- Begin to change these fixed reactions.
- Become freer, more spontaneous, and happier.

The practice of mindfulness was derived from *vipassana*, an Eastern form of meditation that emphasizes the act of quietly sitting and "watching" your breathing, along with any thoughts that might pass through your mind. I like to think of mindfulness practice as a way of creating a little extra space in which your free will can operate. Mindfulness can help you quickly center yourself in the present moment and get away from the mental thoughts and fantasies that tend to pull us all into the past or project us into the future. As you learn how to become an observer of your own thoughts, you'll discover a whole new side of yourself. Worries or fears that would normally cause you to become tense and anxious now just float by and eventually disappear without automatically triggering your habitual defensive reactions. Happy or self-empowering thoughts can be savored and enjoyed, rather than being compulsively pushed off to the side.

We put a heavy emphasis on helping you learn to relax yourself at will. The following statements are typical initial reactions to these exercises:

- "What has this got to do with my cybersex problem?"
- "I already know how to relax, in fact, my partner and I tend to fall asleep too easily!"
- "This is a waste of time. . . . I want to get on to the real stuff."
- "I'm bored."

Breathing *does* seem like a rather odd thing to teach. After all, where would any of us be without it? It stands to reason that we must already "know how" to breathe! Yet, in fact, breathing and relaxation are an integral part of our being in touch with our own bodily feelings; of being able to remain "centered" in ourselves and tune out distractions; and of having the ability to abandon ourselves and all of our senses to our feelings and experience the moment. All of these factors are important to optimal sexual experience and functioning.

Think about the following:

- How often do you find yourself completely open to and experiencing all of the feelings going on in your body at a given moment . . . especially the small quiet ones?
- How often are you able to tune out all thoughts and concerns about work or other interests and completely abandon yourself to your sexual experience with your partner?
- Are you aware of holding your breath at times when you are excited? Angry? Scared?
- How often do you get so tense at work that you can't think straight or solve the problem that's right in front of you?
- How often do you arrive home from work carrying the tensions of the day with you and getting your home life off to a bad start?
- When you stop for a moment to take a few deep, full breaths, do you experience yourself feeling more calm or at ease?

If you are not aware of these things, try watching your reactions to various situations for a few days and notice your own breathing-relaxing patterns.

Exercise 10: The Mindfulness Exercise

This exercise is one that we hope you will include in your daily routine. You may wish to experiment a bit to find the method that works best for you. It is suggested that you begin by allowing yourself at least one-half hour in order to bring yourself to complete relaxation. In time, you may find that it does not take this long. If, in fact, you find it very difficult to take a full half hour for the exercise, we suggest you take whatever time you can find during the day, but then do the exercise more often. For example, if all you can seem to squeeze out of your schedule without interruption is ten minutes, then take ten minutes three times a day. It is important that you get into the habit of doing the exercise daily, and at least once per week take the full block of time at one stretch.

You might also try doing the relaxation exercises at different times of the day—before going to work, during lunch break, before dinner, and so on. For the longer session, though, you will want to have your special, quiet, private space with room to stretch out completely. We also suggest that you get into the habit of doing a relaxation exercise before going on to do other homework tasks for your group.

Sometimes you may prefer to do this exercise alone, while at other times, you and your partner may decide to do it together.

What to do:
- Arrange a space for yourself where you can be alone and quiet.
- Your space must allow you to get into a comfortable position, either lying down flat or sitting up with your spine straight.
- It's preferable to have the lights dim.
- Advise your partner, the kids, and anyone else who may be around that you do not wish to be disturbed for this time. By advising others, you can be freed of responsibility for answering telephones, and so forth.

Abdominal breathing:

- Close your eyes.
- Breathe slowly and evenly, inhaling through your nose deeply and fully, letting the breath go all the way down into your abdomen. (If you place your hand on your stomach, you will feel it fill out.) How often do you let yourself do this? Are you conscious of your stomach sticking out?
- Now exhale, pushing all the air out with your abdomen. Let it come out with a sigh, more fully exhaling than you normally would do.
- Pause a moment after exhaling and then inhale deeply again.
- Do this consciously ten times—feel yourself relax and let yourself continue to relax, breathing deeply and slowly as feels best to you.

Eventually you'll be able to use the breathing or mindfulness exercises anytime, day or night—while driving or working or in the midst of an argument or discussion. You'll find it makes life more livable and gives you more breathing room to make careful, informed decisions rather than tense, knee-jerk ones!

The true motives of our actions, like the real pipes of an organ,
are usually concealed;
but the gilded and hollow pretext is pompously placed in the front for show.

—Charles Caleb Colton

The Six Stages of Recovery

Some aspects of recovery address basic developmental issues, and these issues take time to heal. How much time depends on each person. For some, it may be a year or two, while for others it may be longer. The process is not identical for everyone. Some people have great difficulty stopping their behavior. Be aware that there are critical factors that help the process and others that undermine it, and we'll examine them in the next chapter. At this point, we will explore the six stages that people with compulsive or addictive behaviors go through as they succeed in their recovery.[4]

Keep in mind Hermes' Web and the importance of trying to maintain balance in your life. Be patient. Include others in your recovery. Don't despair at setbacks. Seek help from others.

1. The Developing Stage

Adam was an executive responsible for some of the largest and most important accounts for his high-profile ad agency. He had it all—money, prestige, authority, responsibility—and a secret cybersex life. Adam initially began using the Internet for sex when he discovered online strip clubs. Adam tells his story:

> *I'd often gone to real strip clubs in the past, but as my responsibilities in the agency increased, I just didn't have time to go anymore. The online clubs turned out to be a great substitute. In some ways, I enjoyed them even more than the real thing. I could "visit" whenever I wanted right from my office, and I could actually request specific women and activities. Eventually, I also discovered that I could find and book prostitutes online, too, which I did from both my work and home computers. My life was one of extremes. On the one hand, I managed ad campaigns for women's health care products and, on the other, I abused women through my use of prostitutes.*

One doesn't have to be a high-powered executive to have the addictive pride that says you can manage the unmanageable, that you can do things others can't. It is this arrogance that pushes aside realities like AIDS, family commitments, and work priorities.

Things come apart, however, no matter who you are. For Adam, life began unraveling when his wife stumbled across one of the prostitution booking sites in his computer's history file. Confronted by this undeniable evidence, Adam confessed, but minimized the problem, saying that he'd only gone to the site to see if one could really hire a prostitute online. He swore to his wife that he'd been faithful and to himself that he'd change his ways. Adam even talked about seeing a counselor, but he had not accepted that he had a problem—or at least one he couldn't handle.

Adam was, at this point, in the developing stage. Unmanageability and powerlessness forced him to acknowledge his problem, but he continued his problematic sexual behaviors nonetheless. True recovery begins only after this stage, which can sometimes last two or more years. For Adam, it took more than a year, and, like many others, he made efforts to curtail his activities but his compulsive cybersex behavior continued.

Here are the key characteristics of the Developing Stage:

- seeking help but discontinuing it or deciding it isn't useful

- a growing appreciation of the reality of the problem but a tendency to counter this realization by minimizing the problem or thinking you can handle it by yourself

- temporarily curtailing or stopping the compulsive behavior or substituting other behaviors (Adam delved into sexualized online chat rooms)

- having the fear that stopping cybersex activities would mean stopping sex altogether

For most people struggling with compulsive or addictive sexual behaviors, these behaviors are seen as closely connected to survival. The behavior has until now been a "trusted friend," relied upon for some time. This "friend" has always delivered what it promised, but at a price. As the price grows intolerable, addicts prepare to face the fact that something in their lives has to change.

2. Crisis and Decision

It was three months after Adam gave up his cybersex activities when he felt that life was once again under control.

> One afternoon at work after everyone had left the office for the day, I went online to hire a prostitute. When my colleague's phone rang, I decided to answer it. I left my computer with the "order" information and a photo on my screen. While I was away, my boss returned unexpectedly for some papers he'd forgotten for a meeting. Noticing that the light in my office was still on, he stepped into my office to say hello, but was greeted instead by my computer screen with the prostitution booking service on it—in full view. Caught a second time, and confronted by both my wife and my boss, I

agreed to seek counseling. Since neither could be conned or forced to budge, I finally had to be honest with myself.

Adam had entered the crisis/decision stage, the stage at which a commitment to change is made. This stage can occur within a single day or it can take some months; in any case, it marks the real beginning of recovery. Reaching this stage can happen in many ways. For some, there is a growing consciousness that something needs to be done. Others are frightened into action by the escalation of their behavior. Still others are so overwhelmed by their behavior that they will do anything to fix it.

Most people struggling with compulsive or addictive online sexual behavior were forced to do something by events or by people—family members, partners, friends, or therapists. Because of their denial, the pressure may have had to build up over a long period of time.

3. Shock

This stage is a time of emotional numbness, extraordinary disorientation, and efforts to control the damage. It's not unusual to spend some months in shock. It's okay to move ahead slowly. Maybe nothing major will happen for some time, even for as long as a year. Simply entering recovery and dealing with the implications of the problem can be so stressful that undertaking significant change would overload you. Time-honored sayings like "One day at a time" and "Keep it simple" are appropriate prescriptions for this stage of recovery.

The following experiences can characterize this stage:

- disorientation, confusion, numbness, and an inability to focus or concentrate
- periodic bouts with despair and feelings of hopelessness that can become more intense as the sense of reality grows
- angry feelings about limits set by therapists, sponsors, or family members
- in recovery or support groups, experiencing a sense of belonging along with the realization that recovery was the right decision
- feelings of relief and acceptance once the double life has ended

Perhaps the biggest struggle during this period is for people to be honest with themselves about the extent and nature of their problem. Adam, like many others, began to bargain and argue about his problem. He said:

I remember how intellectual I was and how argumentative I was. As I look back on some of the arguments and discussions I had, the only problematic behavior I admitted was the use of prostitutes. All the other stuff, the lying, the deceit, the chat rooms, the online strip clubs, and other online stuff—I didn't take responsibility for any of that. The fact that I'd been caught was the problem for me.

With time and support, however, clarity about the problematic behavior will emerge. When you can see and accept reality, you will enter a state of profound grieving.

4. Grief

Grieving involves denial or bargaining, anger over the losses, acceptance of the reality of your situation, and sadness. Actually, some aspects of grieving, particularly bargaining and anger, first emerge in earlier stages and simply continue in the grief stage. What really distinguishes this stage is the sadness and pain felt when losses are finally acknowledged.

Given the difficulty of this stage, it shouldn't come as any surprise that this is the point when people most often give up and revert to their old behaviors. Those behaviors had long been used to avoid pain, so when the pain becomes overwhelming, those problematic behaviors seem to bring relief, just as an old friend brings comfort and aid. This is a time when you will badly need outside support. You may be tempted to avoid this pain, but in order to heal and to begin a new life without the problematic behaviors, you simply have to pass through it. It is this pain that sets the stage for the next step; without it, you simply can't take that step.

Here are some of the feelings you may experience during the Grief Stage:

- continued anger and defiance
- sadness and pain punctuated with periodic bouts of despair
- deep sadness over the losses incurred because of your behaviors
- a sense of profound loss as your problematic behaviors cease to serve as friend, comforter, and high

At this point, Adam finally began to see what he'd been doing:

I realized that my getting caught wasn't just bad luck; I realized that I had set these lessons up. The universe kept putting these lessons in front of me and I'd been unwilling to pay attention to them. So the lessons had to get even more dramatic in order for me to finally say, "Okay, I give up. I see the lesson. I'm ready to learn."

When that final acceptance occurs and you allow yourself to be vulnerable—to be human, ordinary, not unique—then significant change can begin. Awareness of your behaviors will expand and deepen over the years. Right now, however, it's important that you recognize its broad outlines and understand that your problem was more than just your behavior. It's important to see that these behaviors grew out of your beliefs, attitudes, and distorted thinking and were preserved with denial and delusion. With acceptance, you then enter the repair stage.

5. Repair

For Adam, the real watershed between grief and repair came when he finally told his wife and his sponsor the true extent of his behaviors and asked from his heart for forgiveness and the opportunity to begin anew.

That is when the chaos stopped and the rebuilding began. Adam began to build "sobriety." He no longer sought out prostitutes or used the Internet for sex:

By this time, I was connected. I was part of a good support group, and I really used the help that they offered daily. We did things socially and I involved myself in meetings—and eventually as a sponsor for another guy who needed help. I immersed myself in therapy, including a weekly men's group. The result was that I was able to set aside my old behavior. I found that my relationship with my wife entered a new and deeply connected level and that I felt for the first time in my life "a sense of spiritual connectedness."

For many, the repair stage is generally marked by the cessation of problematic sexual behaviors, intense spirituality, and personal growth. Adam likened the steps he'd been taking to building the foundation for a new home:

It's brick, sunk in the ground, nothing fancy, just gray, cement blocks. And there's the beginning of a house on top that is in three dimensions and color. I'm not exactly sure what the house will look like, but I can tell already that I'm going to like it.

A number of crucial changes characterize this stage:

- a sense of productivity and renewal
- a new capacity for joy
- deepening new bonds with others
- taking responsibility for yourself in all areas of life, including career, finances, and health
- learning to express your needs, accepting that you have them, and working to meet them
- a focus on completing tasks (degrees, projects, work, and so on) and being dependable (punctual, following through, and responding to requests)
- living less "on the edge and at the extremes"

A common goal at this point is to achieve balance, to learn to live in the balance point of Hermes' Web. Since life has been out of control for so long, you must now focus on the basics. Working toward completion and staying low-key will feel good after all the unmanageability you've experienced. But the repair stage also requires developing new skills and forging new bonds. You will likely be forced to face fundamental issues that made you vulnerable to the draw of cybersex in the first place. Those behaviors can be stopped, but the deeply personal problems of distrust, victimization, and shame will remain. Few people are successful in dealing with them on their own, and it's for this reason that we again strongly urge you to seek therapy and group support.

During this period of repair and personal growth, a greater understanding of your problematic behaviors will continue to grow. Essentially, you will be restructuring your relationship with yourself. You will begin to develop a much better understanding of your behavior and will come to realize what made you vulnerable to cybersex. You will be able to identify the governing themes and scenarios that connect all your problematic behaviors. Once you have a relationship with yourself, you will be able to trust other people. You may also find yourself beginning to trust in a power greater than yourself, a Higher Power, and at that point a spiritual opening occurs. You will no longer be living in fear. You will acquire a vital perspective on your powerlessness, become more forgiving of yourself, and learn to care for yourself more deeply. And at this level of self-care, you will begin to nurture yourself into the growth stage.

6. Growth

Empowered by recovery, you will enter a stage in which you explore new options and restructure relationships. The changes that have occurred will enable you to open up what has been a closed system. Your problematic or addictive behaviors offered only decreasing options. Recovery creates an open personal system that allows for the expansion of countless options. Even better, once a system is open, it has the capacity to renew itself. Many people experience periods of dramatic personal growth years after their initial recovery.

Relationships with children, parents, and partners can all become richer and more sustaining. Many recovering people talk about being more emotionally present on the job, as well. They talk of more balance and greater intimacy, of an improved capacity to resolve conflict, and of being less judgmental and more compassionate. With the evolution of this new style of relationships, satisfaction with life dramatically improves.

Adam experienced these changes, too: "The whole addiction was about me, me, me, me, me. In recovery, I turned to the opposite extreme of really taking care of 'me' in a healthy sense. Then I learned to be a conduit to allow this love that I'm receiving to flow through to others." Adam was very clear about the importance of creating a solid personal base. Of his relationship with his wife, he says, "It is now two wholes sharing a life together."

Characteristics of the growth stage include the following:

- profound empathy and compassion for oneself and for others
- developing trust for one's own boundaries and integrity in relationships
- feelings of achievement over new milestones in love and sex
- a new ability to take care of and nurture relationships
- transforming or ending old relationships

Another characteristic of this growth stage is a deep abhorrence of one's old behavior. Once people in recovery have enough distance from their old problematic behaviors, they often have extremely visceral reactions when they think about them. Many say they look back almost in disbelief at some of the things they've done.

The growth stage provides a special perspective on the course of recovery in general. It's clear that many people with problematic or addictive sexual behaviors were not always able to stop all their behaviors at once. Most people tend to focus initially on what got them into trouble. Then, as their awareness grows, they see the variations on the theme. Recovery moves them from crisis management to an expanded awareness and a more evolved consciousness. And this evolution takes time.

By the time recovery reaches the growth stage, it no longer involves false starts. Consciousness of sobriety and of richer relationships have brought the person to a new level of being. And it's at this stage that people in recovery often talk about the compulsive or addictive behavior as a gift. They have experienced a depth of humanity that many people never achieve. Their compulsive or addictive behaviors and subsequent recovery have given them a greater perception, compassion, and presence. They not only serve as models for other recovering people who follow them, but are literally helping our whole society heal.

In this chapter, you have learned about the four arms of Hermes' Web and the important areas of recovery they represent: relationships, sexuality, spirituality, and self-awareness. This chapter's exercises helped you explore these areas more deeply. As you move further ahead in recovery, you will find that working on them by yourself will be valuable, and we again strongly encourage you to share your work with your therapist and sponsor. In the next chapter, we will introduce you to the RecoveryHex and provide you with more valuable support for your recovery.

CHAPTER 7: *Hope and Recovery*

In the beginning of this workbook, we introduced you to the concept of the CyberHex: six attributes that comprise the Internet and that, when taken together, make it unique among all other media. These six attributes are Intoxicating, Isolating, Integral, Inexpensive, Imposing, and Interactive. We've also talked about how the CyberHex attributes play a role in making the Internet enormously alluring for someone seeking sexual arousal and fulfillment. While any one of these six attributes can be powerful enough to entice a person into the Internet, it is often a combination of these six that draws cybersex users into a ritual of sexually acting out on the Internet.

Fortunately, an even more powerful "RecoveryHex" also exists. As you begin and continue in recovery, you will begin to experience the six attributes of the RecoveryHex. You will discover that the "hex" recovery puts on you will lead you into a life that is richer and more fulfilling than you could have imagined. And best of all, this life is *real*.

As you continue recovery, the RecoveryHex will lead you to greater Insight, to develop greater Intelligence, Integrity, and Influence, to grow as an Individual, and to experience Inspiration.

Insight

When you were immersed in cybersex, your life had a very narrow focus. Much of your time and mental energy revolved around these behaviors: Can I find another great Web site? Will I finally meet the guy of my dreams? How can I be online without getting caught? How can I hide my Internet charges from my partner? And on and on and on.

Once you begin recovery, you will realize that you are no longer focused on your obsessions. You've begun to let other people into your life, you're going to group meetings, you're talking with your therapist, you're renewing friendships. All these changes are helping you focus on yourself in a new, positive way. Your self-awareness is expanding. Like peeling away the layers of an onion, recovery peels away your denial and allows you to see the person you are. Though it may be uncomfortable at first, you may begin to understand why you've acted in a particular way for so long, or why certain situations have always made you uncomfortable, or why you think the way you do.

Once the hex of cybersex is broken, you begin to have what psychologists call "ah-ha!" experiences—flashes of insight that allow you to see yourself, your actions, other people, and the world around you in a new way.

Recovery gives you the ability to live more consciously. Your new self-awareness and insight makes you less susceptible to the spell of the CyberHex because you're now more aware of why it had its hold on you. Your expanded insight enables you to make more conscious decisions.

Even better, these changes are just the beginnings of what can be a lifelong process of personal growth and discovery, one through which you'll continue to develop greater insight and understanding about yourself. This, in turn, will enable you to make healthier decisions.

Intelligence

As your insight deepens, you will find that your emotional intelligence is growing as well. You are more aware of your emotions and better able to manage them. Now, when you are stressed, anxious, sad, or angry, you'll recognize that turning to cybersex behaviors is an ineffective way to deal with such feelings. You're able to say, "I don't want to do that, because the consequences are not going to be worth the price."

Emotional intelligence allows you to "work smarter, not harder." When you were stuck in your compulsive and addictive behaviors, you probably often felt as though you were running a hundred miles an hour in the wrong direction. When faced with a challenge, your emotional intelligence allows you to pause and decide what direction you want to take in order to keep balance in your life. And it helps you marshal your emotions to move in the direction of your goal. Finally, your emotional intelligence helps you become more empathetic toward others, thus making your relationships less troubled and more fulfilling.

Integrity

To have integrity means to strictly hold to a code or standard of values. You may feel bad about your cybersex behaviors and about all that you had to do to hide them from others. No doubt there were lies and deceptions. No matter how far down the scale you've slid, no matter how bad the things were that you've done, you can reclaim yourself—by reclaiming your integrity.

One of your goals in recovery is to define your values and then create a set of guidelines to live by that reflect those values. The First Order changes you initially put in place were the first step in this process. You "drew a line in the sand," so to speak, when you said, "Here are some behaviors I simply will no longer do." You are learning to be rigorously honest with yourself and with everyone in your life. You are learning how to take a stand for what you believe in by living in a certain way. You are not engaging in cybersex any longer. You are being more open with others. Integrity is the ladder out of the black hole of cybersex in which you've been living. And once you experience what it feels like to live with integrity, you will find it more and more difficult to live in any other way.

Influence

Through the process of interacting with others, as the social beings we are, we influence those with whom we're in contact. When you were immersed in cybersex and cut off from others, your influence on those in your life decreased dramatically. And the little that remained was negative.

Recovery is changing all that. Your new influence first extends to you! With greater self-awareness and insight, you can now evaluate the options that come to you in day-to-day life and make better choices and decisions. As you more clearly define who you are as a person, that new "you" will have an effect on others. People will know who you really are and what you stand for. You can have a more positive effect on everyone you meet. You can be a more effective parent. You will have more influence on your children because they will have more respect for you. The same will be true with your spouse or partner, with friends, and with work colleagues.

Individuation

When you become immersed in cybersex, you lose your sense of who you are as a person. Your whole world becomes cybersex—thinking about it, planning for it, doing it, and recovering from it. Your focus becomes sexual gratification. You lose touch with many parts of your self: your role as parent, as spouse or partner, as friend or colleague. You become isolated and lost in the Net, just one of millions of cyber-surfers doing little but staring at a computer monitor.

This aspect of the RecoveryHex helps you begin a process through which you once again become differentiated from others. You begin to regain a sense of the total person you are. You rejoin the world and renew relationships—but this time with insight and awareness of who you are as a human being.

Inspiration

Immersion in compulsive and addictive cybersex behaviors can affect you in many ways. One of these is a physical numbing effect—the result of little or no exercise and sitting for countless hours in front of a computer monitor. A psychological numbing also takes place. You've spent so much mental and emotional energy on your cybersex life that you've got none left for anything else. All of it has been put into getting your cybersex "fix," coming down from it, and working on getting the next one. Other interests atrophy, and life becomes heavy and narrow.

Through the tasks of recovery, you begin to reclaim your life. First of all, the absence of cybersex opens up huge amounts of time for other pursuits. You have choices in what you can do with your time. Without cybersex activities devouring so much of your mental, emotional, and physical energy, you begin to feel hope again. Life seems worth living, and as a result, you feel inspired—inspired to explore your newfound self, to revitalize old relationships and build new ones, to focus again on family and career . . . and much more. Just to discover that you have much to live for is inspiring, in and of itself.

Looking Ahead

In the midst of your compulsive cybersex behaviors, you probably felt many times that cybersex was stronger than you. But now you know differently. You have begun to gain ground. You've stopped your behaviors for now, and you're learning how to make that change permanent.

We caution you not to be overconfident and to continue the work you've begun. If you are seeing a therapist, we urge you to continue doing so. Continue to meet with your Twelve Step group or other support group.

Now that you are finishing this workbook, we want to make another suggestion: go back and review the work you've done. Rereading a good novel always brings to light information and nuances that were missed during the first reading. Likewise with this workbook. You are not the same person today that you were the day you began chapter 1. Rereading the text and reviewing your work in the exercises will give you new insights. Reviewing the exercises on powerlessness, unmanageability, and consequences, for example, will help you see how far you've come, inspire you, and strengthen your resolve to continue your recovery journey. Some exercises may have been very painful for you, and some you may even have skipped. Perhaps now you could move through them, feeling less pain and learning more about yourself.

And yes, you may slip and stumble, but remember that recovery is about progress, not perfection.

Ten Relapse Pitfalls

Beware of these pitfalls as you move further into recovery. Even though you're gaining more insight and understanding about yourself and your behavior, the recovery road is not a smooth superhighway. There are potholes ahead, but you can avoid them, especially if you know what to watch out for. Here are ten to beware of—and suggestions for bypassing them "unharmed."

Now that the crisis is over, there's no longer a problem.

This pitfall is common because it's tempting to think this way after your initial crisis has passed. After that chaos, the First Order changes you put in place make your life feel almost carefree. It will seem as though the problem is solved.

Well, it isn't. You've only dealt with crisis management; you still must deal with all the factors that led you into compulsive or addictive cybersex in the first place. And this takes time. And effort. And the help of others. This is a lifelong issue that you will always need to be aware of and to manage. As time passes and your recovery strengthens, less vigilance will be needed, of course, but the potential for relapse will always remain.

Chaos helps me remember I'm alive.

It is not unusual for people who are involved in addictive or compulsive behavior to like the drama of crisis. And because they like it, "calm" isn't comfortable. It doesn't feel "right"—because they are accustomed to crises and the adrenaline rush that they bring on. If you're not familiar with life feeling calm, you may be tempted to create a situation in which a crisis will occur.

At times like this, you would do well to tell yourself the following: Crisis isn't common; calm is okay. Yes, calm is okay. Life in recovery will feel different from life overwhelmed by cybersex, but just because it feels different or makes you uncomfortable doesn't mean it's bad. In fact, calm indicates that you have begun to create balance in your life. Life in crisis is life out of balance.

It's also common for people who are involved in addictive or compulsive behavior to think that a life without it will be boring—that they won't have any fun or excitement anymore. But thinking about your cybersex-obsessed life as being "fun and exciting" is not accurate—just review your consequences list for a reality check. As time passes, you *will* find much in your life that's interesting, exciting, and fun. You may even see your ability to manage and control your life as "fun."

I'll start feeling better immediately.

As you begin recovery, you may expect to feel better immediately. Yes, once you've gotten First Order changes in place, you should feel some immediate relief. Once you begin the Transition and especially the Second Order changes, life may seem more difficult again—although in a different way than when you were doing cybersex. Strong feelings such as sadness, grief, anger, shame, regret, and failure may surface and cause great discomfort. You will likely feel worse again before turning the corner toward truly brighter days. Our culture teaches us to expect quick fixes for our problems: Pop a pill to take care of pain—either physical or emotional—and it will be gone. Recovery—which means making fundamental changes in ourselves and our lives—is neither easy and quick, nor is it pain-free. But when you persevere, the rewards can be remarkable.

I'll be able to handle or manage sex on the Internet.

Once people have progressed in recovery, they can reach a point at which it is tempting to say, "I can handle this," while dabbling in the problematic behavior. An alcoholic may say, "I've been sober for quite some time. I've finally got this drinking issue under control. It's now safe for me to have a drink once in a while." The same can be said for someone who's been engaged in cybersex.

"I had been in recovery from cybersex for nearly two years," said Terrence, a prominent lawyer. "One of the steps I'd taken was not to have the password to my computer. After this amount of time, I really felt I didn't need this safeguard any longer and convinced my wife to reveal it to me. Sad to say, within six months, I was back in trouble with cybersex again."

Don't fall into this pit. This kind of thinking is really no more than bargaining with your compulsion—"I'll give up nearly all these behaviors, but not all"—in an attempt to avoid the feelings of grief and loss over truly letting go of your problematic behaviors. This pitfall is really an attempt to find ways that you can actually do the cybersex behavior without losing your sobriety totally. When you truly admit that you can't handle cybersex, then you will have to deal with painful feelings about losing that activity in your life.

This kind of self-talk is very seductive and it's possible that, at some point, you will go back to cybersex and soon find yourself in full relapse. If you do, try not to despair. Look at it as a lesson that needed to be learned, and then move on.

To remind yourself of just how much "control" you really had, review the cybersex log you did in chapter 2 and your powerlessness and unmanageability lists in chapter 5. We also strongly suggest that when you find yourself thinking such thoughts, contact your sponsor, a support group member, or your therapist immediately.

It wasn't that bad when I was doing it.

This pitfall is similar to the previous one. It's the result of a condition we call "addiction amnesia." After you have been in recovery for some time, a voice in your head will make statements like, "Doing what I did really wasn't that bad," or "I really didn't have too many consequences," or "I didn't have consequences that I couldn't handle."

When such thoughts surface, you need to do a reality check. Again, you might review the consequences list in chapter 5, and when you do, you'll quickly see just how bad the consequences of your cybersex behaviors were. Look at the cybersex log you completed in chapter 2. You might also ask your spouse, partner, or someone else whose life was affected by your behaviors just how great the problem was. Ask them how they were affected.

This problem is different for me than it is for others.

This kind of thinking is likely to arise once you begin attending a support group or Twelve Step group. After hearing many people's stories, you may find yourself thinking that your situation is unique, that your problem is either worse or less serious than anyone else's. If you think that you're better than the others and that your situation is not very serious, you aren't accepting the true extent of your problem—and you're more likely to relapse. On the other hand, if you begin to believe that you're worse off than everyone else, you are likely to trigger your feelings of shame. You may then tell yourself that you'll never be able to control your cybersex behaviors anyway, so why even bother trying to stop?

The pitfall here is "unique thinking"—believing you're different from other people. Comparing your situation with that of others is pointless. Severity is irrelevant. You all have the same problem and you all need to stay in recovery.

A slip (or relapse) equals a failure, so why continue recovery?

Let's say you're on a diet. You've lost twelve pounds already, but you are still a bit less than halfway to your weight goal. One evening you're visiting a friend's home and she offers you some Oreo cookies. You know you should decline, but you take and eat three anyway. Later, you're in the kitchen by yourself when you discover a cookie jar filled with more Oreos. You think, "What the heck, I've slipped already so I might as well eat all of these that I can." Is eating three, a small slip, a good reason to go back and eat the rest of the bag?

Slips and relapse are often part of recovery. Think about the stages of change that we discussed in chapter 3. Do you remember how the process sometimes means taking a few steps backward before permanently moving ahead? Having a slip is not reason for despair, nor is it a justification for surrendering to your compulsive and addictive behaviors again. You've made progress in your recovery. Much good has happened. You slipped, so get up, brush yourself off, and get back on the path. Then, talk with your sponsor or therapist about what happened and develop a plan for avoiding such a slip or relapse in the future.

I can't do recovery for the rest of my life; therefore, there's no hope for me.

Particularly in early recovery after that first rush of good feelings has passed and suddenly things look much more difficult again, you may say something like this to yourself: "Oh, my God, I've been struggling with this for six weeks. It's so hard. I can't even imagine going through this for the rest of my life! There's really no hope."

Many, many people in recovery have had such thoughts. They are typical of early recovery. What you need to do is to turn your focus away from the future and stay in the present. Right now, you are not involved in cybersex behaviors. Take life one minute, one hour, one day at a time. Recovery does become easier with time—and not just because you're "stronger," but because it feels better and better to be in recovery. Your life begins to have more joy. You begin to feel the reinforcement of the RecoveryHex—insight, intelligence, integrity, influence, individuation, and inspiration. Recovery is something you want because it's making your life better. And soon, all those "one day at a times" turn into weeks and months and even years. Pay attention to today; the future will take care of itself.

I can do this on my own.

"I don't need other people to help me." "I don't need God or a spiritual connection that people talk about." "I'm strong; I can do this on my own."

This kind of thinking indicates that you have not moved beyond First Order change. You were isolated in your cybersex behaviors, and now you are still isolated in your recovery. Isolation will draw you back into your compulsive or addictive behaviors.

As we have emphasized throughout this workbook, you cannot recover on your own. You need others to take this path successfully. People are ready to help you. You need only ask. In fact, by not allowing other people to help, you are actually denying them an opportunity to give you a gift.

My partner didn't leave me, so what I did couldn't have been so bad for him (her).

Just because your partner or spouse—or friends and colleagues—didn't completely abandon you does not mean that your behaviors didn't hurt them. Forgiveness does not mean permission to return to your compulsive behaviors. Forgiveness is based on the hope and the promise you've made to work on your behavior and not repeat your mistakes.

When you find yourself thinking like this, we suggest that you talk with the people in your life who were affected by your cybersex behaviors and ask them to tell you how they were affected. As time passes, you may forget what happened (again, this is addiction amnesia). While there's no need to revisit the past regularly, it is useful to occasionally remember when you were so out of control, when people were upset with you and you were creating havoc in your life and the lives of others. Bringing that time to light serves as an effective remedy for this kind of thinking.

Twelve Step groups and support groups are effective in part because they also serve as a means of reminding members of what a life of compulsion and addiction is like. When newcomers join and tell their story, all are reminded of the place they once lived and how far they've come.

More Relapse Traps

Here are four problem attitudes that we call tried-and-true relapse traps: entitlement, resentment, deprivation, and stress. Getting them out in the open will help you avoid relapse.

Entitlement

People who fail at some task, who are struggling with problems, or who feel put upon often feel so much self-pity that they believe they are entitled to some kind of reward for their struggles. In addition, people who are very accomplished and overreach themselves can likewise feel that they deserve some reward for all their hard work. Many people who struggle with compulsive and addictive behaviors stretch their lives to the extreme. They often have a difficult time saying no to others' requests and find themselves overcommitted. Ministry and medicine, for example, are two professions that reinforce overcommitted behaviors. The people who are drawn to these professions are often very good at it and committed to helping others, repeatedly giving in positive ways, but they also often do a poor job of taking care of their own needs. It then becomes easy for them to think that, because they work so hard for others, they are entitled to some reward, and some "rewards," such as cybersex or affairs, can be very self-destructive. Their feelings of entitlement don't derive from a sense of narcissism; instead they grow out of an inability to say no to the needs of others.

Resentment

During the recovery process, it's common for feelings of anger and resentment to surface. These feelings may come from many sources: resentment about difficult predicaments, losses suffered, past and future consequences of out-of-bounds behavior, family-of-origin issues, and so on. It is important to acknowledge and address these feelings with a therapist or sponsor. If they remain unaddressed, they can lead to ever stronger feelings of self-pity and entitlement—and eventually to relapse.

Deprivation: Abstaining from All Things Sexual

In recovery from any problematic sexual behavior, it is tempting to say to yourself, "That's it. I'm just going off sex. It's caused me so much trouble, and I don't seem to know how to handle it in a healthy way. I'm just going to quit." The problem is that you can't quit being sexual, and, more important, you don't have to. Trying to abstain will only set you up for a relapse. Many people who are on food diets experience similar problems. They diet carefully, denying in the process all the foods they really like. The result? Inevitably they leave their diet behind, only to fall into eating binges and regaining the lost weight. "Entitlement" thinking plays a key role here, too. When dieting, it's easy to tell yourself that you've been good for so long and you've deprived yourself of the foods you love for so long that you're now entitled to engage in the "forbidden" loves. That's relapse. If you live in a state of deprivation, you will be more vulnerable to feelings of entitlement. It works the same way with sex.

People who successfully lose weight instead learn how to eat healthfully. They also take the time and effort to look inside themselves to see what emotional needs or family issues lie behind their habit of overeating, and they make plans to deal with the cravings that will inevitably arise.

Successful recovery from your dysfunctional cybersex behaviors won't happen through sexual abstinence but instead through following the steps we have laid out, in particular the Second Order changes you make. These steps lead to personal awareness and growth, to an ability to nurture yourself, to intimacy with those you love, and to a healthy sexuality in which you will no longer need your old behaviors to feel good.

Simply stopping problematic or addictive behaviors does not equate with recovery. Again, we are talking about making only First Order changes. Without the introspection and inner growth that come with Second Order changes, you are merely setting yourself up for relapse. Feelings of deprivation and entitlement will surely arise. And you may find yourself engaging in compulsive behaviors of another kind, such as drinking or gambling. Until the issues underlying your problematic or addictive sexual behaviors are addressed, there will be no recovery.

Stress

Higher-than-normal stress levels can quickly increase your risk of relapse. Remember, too, that stress is not always created by negative situations or events. Receiving a long-sought work promotion, moving to a new city, the birth of a child, or a new relationship can all create stress, too. If you are unsure about ways to handle the stress in your life, seek out a course on stress management skills, relaxation training, or meditation—and then put these skills to use.

Beware of the Bounce Effect

The bounce effect tends to occur after people have been working on their recovery and are attending support groups. They initially make big disclosures as they tell their story and, having done so, they feel better—and then they stop. They don't take further Steps. They rarely call their sponsor. They attend meetings but don't really participate in them.

They have failed to understand that change, growth, and healing are *ongoing* processes and that they need to share continually what is happening in their recovery and lives. Opening up to others is not a one-time event or simply an end in itself. It is the first step in sharing who you are and who you are becoming. This kind of openness needs to become a way of life if you are to succeed in recovery. Research with thousands of recovering people who have participated in Twelve Step programs has shown that those who committed to and followed the program through Step Nine rarely relapse.

The goal of treatment and recovery is not to immediately jump to the other extreme—to make an enormous and dramatic splash at a meeting and to your sponsor and then be done with everything else. Instead, seek the middle ground. Begin the process and then continue it. Participate in your therapy groups, work the Steps of your program, and begin to do service to others. You won't, at this point, know where this will all end, but have faith in the process and continue. Go on sharing your life and your problems and your challenges and your failures with others in your therapy program or recovery group and with your sponsor—and keep coming back week after week, month after month, and year after year.

Recovery is not an event; it is an ongoing process and a process that will, over time, become less focused on recovery from problematic sexual behaviors and more focused on personal and spiritual growth.

Stay Alert for Signs of Trouble

Here are more solid suggestions for preventing relapse. Social pressures, internal challenges, and special situations are common threats to maintenance and recovery. Social pressures come from those around you who either engage in cybersex themselves or don't recognize its impact on your life. Internal challenges usually result from overconfidence and other forms of defective thinking, such as the ten relapse pitfalls and the four relapse traps we discussed above.

While many of the more common temptations will occur for you during the action stage, most people learn to deal with them before moving out of that stage. During maintenance, however, the relatively rarer temptations come into play. They are difficult to anticipate and pose serious threats to your confidence, convictions, and commitment.

Additional Suggestions for Maintaining Commitment and Recovery

- Write down the difficulties you encountered in your early efforts to change your cybersex behaviors. Next, review the lists you made in chapter 5 in which you described the negative aspects of your cybersex behaviors. Keep both of these lists handy, look at them periodically, and refer to them at the first sign of slipping.

- Take credit for your accomplishment. This is not the time to criticize yourself for having had problems; instead take both credit and responsibility for change. Use the new year, your birthday, or the anniversary of your change (it doesn't have to be a year; celebrate month by month at first) to reflect on the success you have had and to renew your commitment.

- As you progress in your recovery, you will gradually become more comfortable in the presence of temptations. But you may not become completely immune to them. Especially during the early months of maintenance, it's best to continue to avoid people, places, or things that could compromise your recovery. Pay attention to the behaviors you need to avoid (found in your recovery-zone plan).

- Keep your intervention cards with you. In addition, you can make a crisis card for your wallet or purse. On it, write a list of the negative consequences of your problem, as well as a set of instructions to follow when you are seriously tempted to slip. The instructions could read as follows: (1) review the negative consequences of the behavior; (2) substitute a positive alternative for the cybersex behavior; (3) remember the benefits of changing; (4) engage in distracting or positive behavior; and (5) call someone (write down a support person's name and phone number).

- Once you have worked your way past the relapse pitfalls and traps, you may believe that you've got them beat. Unfortunately, that may not be the case. It would be unusual if some of them didn't "wake from the dead" in a year or two. Remember that compulsive and addictive behaviors are, in Twelve Step language, cunning, baffling, and powerful. Often, these pitfalls and traps will arise just at the moment you think you're doing well—when you least expect it, in other words. Being aware, however, that they could trouble you again is a key to overcoming them. If you remain vigilant, you're less likely to be caught off guard when they do return.

- Last, but by no means least, seek help and support from your support group, therapist, partner or spouse, and friends. Having someone to call on who has been where you are, who can understand, and who can help is simply invaluable.

Though recovery may seem to be a daunting and endless task, we encourage you to begin thinking in a new way about these changes. If you think of recovery as a burden akin to a diet, it just won't work. Try to view the path on which you've set out as a truly remarkable opportunity, because that is exactly what it is. Once you begin to change, to accept the support others are offering to you, and to live in balance, you will find that you love your new life so much that you don't want to give it up. Gradually, staying in balance will no longer seem like something you have to do, but something you want to do. You will begin to truly cherish what you've found. This newfound caring for yourself and the pride it creates will build a new feeling of being capable—of self-confidence and self-esteem. This is a hope-filled process.

Even if you are not yet at the point where you have started to experience these feelings, it's important that you know that this place exists. If you've read the workbook to this point without having done the work we suggested, you're unlikely to understand or believe that this is possible. But by doing the work, you can get there. This is not a fantasy or an illusion. You can reach a point where you want to be in recovery—a point where your passion for recovery is as strong as your passion for cybersex once was.

The information, suggestions, and guidelines we've provided can help you start on the road to recovery. You *can* recover. You *can* create better relationships and live a richer, more fulfilling life. Reach out to others for strength, support, and encouragement. Everything that you need will be given to you.

The Twelve Steps of Alcoholics Anonymous[1]

1. We admitted we were powerless over alcohol—that our lives had become unmanageable.

2. Came to believe that a Power greater than ourselves could restore us to sanity.

3. Made a decision to turn our will and our lives over to the care of God *as we understood Him.*

4. Made a searching and fearless moral inventory of ourselves.

5. Admitted to God, to ourselves, and to another human being the exact nature of our wrongs.

6. Were entirely ready to have God remove all these defects of character.

7. Humbly asked Him to remove our shortcomings.

8. Made a list of all persons we had harmed, and became willing to make amends to them all.

9. Made direct amends to such people wherever possible, except when to do so would injure them or others.

10. Continued to take personal inventory and when we were wrong promptly admitted it.

11. Sought through prayer and meditation to improve our conscious contact with God *as we understood Him*, praying only for knowledge of His will for us and the power to carry that out.

12. Having had a spiritual awakening as the result of these steps, we tried to carry this message to alcoholics, and to practice these principles in all our affairs.

1. The Twelve Steps of AA are taken from *Alcoholics Anonymous*, 3d ed., published by AA World Services, Inc., New York, N.Y., 59-60.

The Twelve Steps of Alcoholics Anonymous Adapted for Sexual Addicts

1. We admitted we were powerless over our sexual addiction—that our lives had become unmanageable.

2. Came to believe a Power greater than ourselves could restore us to sanity.

3. Made a decision to turn our will and our lives over to the care of God, as we understood Him.

4. Made a searching and fearless moral inventory of ourselves.

5. Admitted to God, to ourselves, and to another human being the exact nature of our wrongs.

6. Were entirely ready to have God remove all these defects of character.

7. Humbly asked Him to remove our shortcomings.

8. Made a list of all persons we had harmed, and became willing to make amends to them all.

9. Made direct amends to such people wherever possible, except when to do so would injure them or others.

10. Continued to take personal inventory and when we were wrong promptly admitted it.

11. Sought through prayer and meditation to improve our conscious contact with God as we understood Him, praying only for knowledge of His will for us and the power to carry that out.

12. Having had a spiritual awakening as the result of these steps, we tried to carry this message to others and to practice these principles in all our affairs.

Resources Guide

Following is a list of recovery fellowships that may be helpful in you.

Adult Children of Alcoholics
310-534-1815
www.adultchildren.org

Alateen (ages 12–17)
800-356-9996
www.al-anon-alateen.org

Al-Anon
800-344-2666
www.al-anon-alateen.org

Alcoholics Anonymous
212-870-3400
www.alcoholics-anonymous.org

Co-Dependents Anonymous
602-277-7991
www.codependents.org

Co-Dependents of Sex Addicts
612-537-6904

Cocaine Anonymous
800-347-8998
www.ca.org

CoAnon
www.co-anon.org

Debtors Anonymous
781-453-2743
www.debtorsanonymous.org

Emotions Anonymous
651-647-9712
www.mtn.org/EA

Families Anonymous
310-815-8010
www.familiesanonymous.org

Gamblers Anonymous
213-386-8789
www.gamblersanonymous.org

Marijuana Anonymous
212-459-4423
www.marijuana-anonymous.org

Narcotics Anonymous
818-773-9999
www.na.org

National Council for Couple and Family Recovery
314-997-9808

National Council on Sexual Addiction and Compulsivity
770-989-9754
www.ncsac.org

Nicotine Anonymous
www.nicotine-anonymous.org

Overeaters Anonymous
www.oa.org

Recovering Couples Anonymous
314-830-2600
www.recovering-couples.org

Recovery Online
www.onlinerecovery.org/index.html

Runaway and Suicide Hotline
800-621-4000

S-Anon
615-833-3152
www.sanon.org

Sex and Love Addicts Anonymous
781-255-8825
www.slaafws.org

Sex Addicts Anonymous
713-869-4902
www.sexaa.org

Sexual Addiction Resources/Dr. Patrick Carnes
www.sexhelp.com

Sexual Compulsives Anonymous
310-859-5585
www.sca-recovery.org

Survivors of Incest Anonymous
410-282-3400

Contact List for More Information

This workbook was written in part to serve as a companion to the book *In the Shadows of the Net: Breaking Free of Compulsive Online Sexual Behavior*, which was written with Patrick Carnes, Ph.D., and is published by Hazelden (www.hazelden.org).

For more information about treatment and recovery services at the Hazelden Foundation, please call 1-800-257-7800, or access them on the Internet at www.hazelden.org.

For information on both inpatient and outpatient treatment and recovery services at The Meadows in Wickenburg, Arizona, contact them at 1-800-MEADOWS.

For more information about Dr. Patrick Carnes and his speaking engagements, access his Web site at www.sexhelp.com or call him at 1-800-708-1796.

For information about Dr. David Delmonico and his speaking engagements, contact him at Duquesne University at 412-396-4032.

For information about Elizabeth Griffin and her speaking engagements, contact her at the American Foundation for Addiction Research at 952-915-9454.

Books of related interest written by Dr. Patrick Carnes

The Betrayal Bond: Breaking Free of Explotive Relationships
(Deerfield Beach, Fla.: Health Communications, 1998)
In a savage psychic twist, victims of abuse and violence often bond with their perpetrators to the stunning point that they will die rather than escape. Carnes's breakthrough book focuses on how betrayal intensifies trauma and illuminates the keys to escaping destructive relationships.

Sexual Anorexia: Overcoming Sexual Self-Hatred (with Joseph Moriarity)
(Center City, Minn.: Hazelden, 1997)
The devastating mix of fear, pain, and betrayal can lead to obsessive sexual aversion. Tracing the dysfunction's roots in childhood sexual trauma, neglect, and abuse, Carnes explores dimensions of sexual health, targeting key issues that let recovery proceed.

Out of the Shadows: Understanding Sexual Addiction, third edition
(Center City, Minn.: Hazelden, 2001)
The groundbreaking book that first identified and defined sexual addiction. A must for anyone looking to understand the illness, it's an expert and in-depth look at the origins of sexual addiction and the addiction cycle.

Facing the Shadows: Beginning Sexual and Relationship Recovery
(Center City, Minn.: Hazelden 2001)
A companion workbook for Carnes's book, *Out of the Shadows*, it takes techniques used by thousands of recovering sex addicts and shows readers, step by step, how to break free of problematic sexual behaviors and live a healthier, more fulfilling life.

Contrary to Love: Helping the Sexual Addict
(Center City, Minn.: Hazelden, 1989)
This sequel *to Out of the Shadows* traces the origins and consequences of the addict's faulty core beliefs. Building upon his earlier work, Carnes describes the stages of the illness and lays the groundwork for potential recovery.

Don't Call It Love: Recovering From Sexual Addiction
(Phoenix, Ariz.: Gentle Path Press, 1991)
This landmark study of one thousand recovering sex addicts and their families explores how people become sex addicts and the role of culture, family, neurochemistry, and child abuse in creating addiction.

A Gentle Path through the Twelve Steps: The Classic Guide for All People in the Process of Recovery
(Center City, Minn.: Hazelden, 1994)
A guidebook for people in recovery that helps them understand their own story and begin planning a new life of recovery. With more than 250,000 copies sold, it holds invaluable insights for beginners and old-timers alike in any Twelve Step program.

VIDEOTAPES BY GENTLE PATH PRESS

For more information or to order videotapes from Gentle Path Press, call 800-708-1796.

Trauma Bonds: When Humans Bond with Those Who Hurt Them
Victims often cling to destructive relationships with baffling desperation. In this riveting videotape, Dr. Patrick Carnes analyzes how trauma bonding develops and outlines strategies for breaking free from its compulsive torment.

Addiction Interaction Disorder: Understanding Multiple Addictions
Few addicts—about 17 percent—have only one addiction. More commonly, assorted compulsions combine in a complex systemic problem called addiction interaction disorder. This tape outlines how to screen for the disorder (a major factor in relapse) and explores the role of addiction as a "solution" to trauma.

Contrary to Love: Helping the Sexual Addict
A twelve-part PBS video in which noted addiction psychologist Dr. Patrick Carnes discusses the spectrum of compulsive-addictive behavior and its treatment. The titles of the twelve parts are
　　"Our Addictive Society"
　　"Cultural Denial of Addiction"
　　"Am I an Addict?"
　　"Interview with Three"
　　"The Addictive Family"
　　"Interview with Melody Beattie"
　　"Child Abuse
　　"The Twelve-Step Recovery Process"
　　"Healthy Sexuality and Spirituality"
　　"Finding a Balance in Recovery"
　　"Coping in a World of Shame"
　　"The Ten Risks of Recovery"

AUDIOCASSETTES BY GENTLE PATH PRESS

For more information or to order audiocassettes from Gentle Path Press, call 800-708-1796.

Trauma Bonds: When We Bond with Those Who Hurt Us
Addiction Interaction Disorder: Understanding Multiple Addictions
Toward a New Freedom: Discovering Healthy Sexuality
Sexual Abuse in the Church
Sexual Dependency, Compulsion and Obsession

For Further Reading

The following list contains books referenced in this book, in addition to further readings that may be helpful.

Cybersex

Carnes, Patrick, David Delmonico, Elizabeth Griffin, Joseph Moriarity. *In the Shadows of the Net: Breaking Free of Compulsive Online Sexual Behavior*. Center City, Minn: Hazelden, 2001. [Ed. note: This workbook was written in part to serve as a companion to the book, *In the Shadows of the Net*, which offers additional information about problematic cybersex behavior and recovery that you will find valuable in your work. Topics in the book that may interest you include the stages of courtship, patterns of sexual arousal and ways they change, setting appropriate relationship boundaries, relapse prevention, the impact of cybersex on the family, and the Web frontier.]

Schneider, Jennifer and Robert Weiss. *Cybersex Exposed: Simple Fantasy or Obsession*. Center City, Minn.: Hazelden, 2001.

Co-Sex Addiction Recovery

Beattie, Melody. *Codependent No More: How to Stop Controlling Others and Start Caring for Yourself*. New York: Walker, 1989.

Calof, David L., and Robin Simons. *The Couple Who Became Each Other and Other Tales of Healing of a Master Hypnotherapist*. New York: Bantam Books, 1996.

Carnes, Patrick J. *The Betrayal Bond: Breaking Free of Exploitive Relationships*. Deerfield Beach, Fla.: Health Communications, 1998.

Fossum, Merle A., and Marilyn J. Mason. *Facing Shame: Families in Recovery*. New York: Norton, 1989.

Friel, John, and Linda Friel. *Adult Children: The Secrets of Dysfunctional Families*. Deerfield Beach, Fla.: Health Communications, 1988.

Schaeffer, Brenda. *Is It Love or Is It Addiction?* 2d ed. Center City, Minn: Hazelden, 1997.

Schneider, Jennifer. *Back from Betrayal: Recovering from His Affairs*. New York: Ballantine Books, 1990.

Schneider, Jennifer P., and Burt Schneider. *Sex, Lies, and Forgiveness: Couples Speaking Out on Healing From Sex Addiction*. Center City, Minn.: Hazelden, 1991.

Family

Bradshaw, John. *Bradshaw on the Family: A Revolutionary Way of Self-Discovery*. Pompano Beach, Fla.: Health Communications, 1988.

Evans, Patricia. *The Verbally Abusive Relationship: How to Recognize It and How to Respond*. Holbrook, Mass.: Adams Media Corporation, 1996.

Love, Patricia. *Emotional Incest Syndrome: What to Do When a Parent's Love Rules Your Life*. New York: Bantam Books, 1991.

Mellody, Pia, with Andrea Well Miller and J. Keith Miller. *Facing Codependence*. San Francisco: Harper San Francisco, 1989.

Key Recovery Works

Beattie, Melody. *Journey to the Heart: Daily Meditations on the Path to Freeing Your Soul*. San Francisco: Harper San Francisco, 1996.

Bradshaw, John. *Healing the Shame That Binds You*. Deerfield Beach, Fla.: Health Communications, 1988.

Breton, Denise, and Christopher Largent. *The Paradigm Conspiracy: Why Our Social Systems Violate Our Human Potential—and How We Can Change Them*. Center City, Minn.: Hazelden, 1996.

Bryan, Mark, and Julia Cameron. *The Money Drunk: Ninety Days to Financial Sobriety*. New York: Ballantine Books, 1993.

Cameron, Julia. *The Artist's Way: A Spiritual Path to Higher Creativity*. New York: Putnam, 1995.

Covey, Stephen R. *First Things First: Everyday*. New York: Simon & Schuster, 1999.

———. *The Seven Habits of Highly Effective People: Powerful Lessons in Personal Change*. New York: Simon & Schuster, 1989.

Hope and Recovery: The Twelve Step Guide for Healing from Compulsive Sexual Behavior. Center City, Minn.: Hazelden, 1994.

Milkman, Harvey B., and Stanley Sunderwirth. *Craving for Ecstasy: The Chemistry and Consciousness of Escape*. New York: Free Press, 1987.

Millman, Dan. *Way of the Peaceful Warrior: A Book That Changes Lives*. Tiburon, Calif.: Kramer, 1984.

Mundis, Jerrold. *How to Get Out of Debt, Stay Out of Debt & Live Prosperously*. New York: Bantam Books, 1990.

Nouwen, Henri J. *Reaching Out: The Three Movements of the Spiritual Life*. Garden City, N.Y.: Doubleday, 1986.

Peck, M. Scott. *People of the Lie: The Hope for Healing Human Evil*. New York: Simon & Schuster, 1985.

———. *The Road Less Traveled*. New York: Simon & Schuster, 1978.

Sex Addiction

Adams, Kenneth M. *Silently Seduced: When Parents Make Their Children Partners*. Deerfield Beach, Fla.: Health Communications, 1991.

Answers in the Heart. Center City, Minn.: Hazelden, 1994.

Earle, Ralph H., and Gregory Crowe. *Lonely All the Time: Recognizing, Understanding, and Overcoming Sex Addiction, for Addicts and Co-Dependents*. n.p.: Bradt, 1998.

Ellison, Marvin M. *Erotic Justice: A Liberating Ethic of Sexuality*. Louisville, Ky.: Westminster John Knox Press, 1996.

Hastings, Anne S. *From Generation to Generation: Learning about Adults Who Are Sexual with Children*. Tiburon, Calif.: Printed Voice, 1994.

Kasl, Charlotte. *Women, Sex, and Addiction*. Harper & Row, 1989.

Nouwen, Henri J. *The Return of the Prodigal Son: A Story of Homecoming*. New York: Doubleday, 1994.

Sexual Health

Bechtal, Stephen. *The Practical Encyclopedia of Sex and Health.* Emmaus, Pa.: Rodale Press, 1993.

Berzon, Betty, ed. *Positively Gay.* Berkeley, Calif.: CelestialArts, 1995.

Covington, Stephanie. *Awakening Your Sexuality: A Guide for Recovering Women.* Center City, Minn.: Hazelden, 1991.

Diamond, Jed. *Male Menopause: Sex and Survival in the Second Half of Life.* Naperville, Ill.: Sourcebooks, 1997.

Eisler, Riane. *The Chalice and the Blade: Our History, Our Future.* San Francisco: Harper & Row, 1987.

Hastings, Anne S. *Discovering Sexuality That Will Satisfy You Both: When Couples Want Differing Amounts and Different Kinds of Sex.* Tiburon, Calif.: Printed Voice, 1993.

Klausner, Mary A., and Bobbie Hasselbring. *Aching for Love: The Sexual Drama of the Adult Child.* San Francisco: Harper San Francisco, 1990.

Maltz, Wendy. *The Sexual Healing Journey: A Guide for Survivors of Sexual Abuse.* New York: HarperCollins, 1991.

———, ed. *Passionate Hearts: The Poetry of Sexual Love.* Novato, Calif.: New World Library, 1997.

Renshaw, Domeena. *Seven Weeks to Better Sex.* New York: Random House, 1995.

Sex and Religion

Elinor, Burkett, and Frank Bruni. *A Gospel of Shame: Children, Sexual Abuse, and the Catholic Church.* New York: Viking Penguin, 1993.

Laaser, Mark. *Faithful and True: Sexual Integrity in a Fallen World.* Grand Rapids, Mich.: Zondervan, 1996.

———, ed. *Restoring the Soul of a Church: Reconciling Congregations Wounded by Clergy Sexual Misconduct.* Collegeville, Minn.: Liturgical Press, 1995.

Rossetti, Stephen J. *A Tragic Grace: The Catholic Church and Child Sexual Abuse.* Collegeville, Minn.: Liturgical Press, 1996.

Sipe, A. W. Richard. *Sex, Priests, and Power: Anatomy of a Crisis.* New York: Brunner/Mazel, 1995.

Trauma Resolution

Bass, Ellen, and Laura Davis. *The Courage to Heal: A Guide for Women Survivors of Child Sexual Abuse.* New York: HarperCollins, 1994.

Courtois, Christine A. *Healing the Incest Wound: Adult Survivors in Therapy.* New York: Norton, 1996.

Crowder, Adrienne. *Opening the Door: A Treatment Model for Therapy with Male Survivors of Sexual Abuse.* Philadelphia: Brunner/Mazel, 1995.

Davis, Laura. *Allies in Healing: When the Person You Love Was Sexually Abused as a Child.* New York: HarperCollins, 1991.

Dolan, Yvonne. *Resolving Sexual Abuse: Solution-Focused Therapy and Ericksonian Hypnosis for Adult Survivors.* New York: Norton, 1991.

Fossum, Merle A., and Marilyn J. Mason. *Facing Shame: Families in Recovery.* New York: Norton, 1986.

Hunter, Mic. *Abused Boys: The Neglected Victims of Sexual Abuse.* New York: Fawcett, 1991.

Maltz, Wendy, and Beverly Holman. *Incest and Sexuality: A Guide to Understanding and Healing.* Lexington, Ky.: Lexington Books, 1987.

Miller, Alice. *For Your Own Good: Hidden Cruelty in Child-Rearing and the Roots of Violence.* New York: Farrar, Straus, Giroux, 1990.

White, William L. *The Incestuous Workplace: Stress and Distress in the Organizational Family.* Center City, Minn.: Hazelden, 1997.

Hermes' Web and the Web Sight Program

Hermes' Web
- is an innovative new tool for working with difficult clients
- helps communicate essential psychological concepts
- demonstrates treatment dynamics
- compensates for learning and comprehension difficulties
- helps build the connection between intention and behavior
- meets clients where they are—dubbed "the equalizer"
- works on multichannels: visual, tactile, abstract, spiritual
- can be used with many treatment models and modalities

Hermes' Web, Ltd., also offers The Web Sight Program, which incorporates the use of The Web. The Web Sight Program is unique—it combines ten essential and difficult components which, when brought together, have the capacity to reach, work with, and affect the most difficult clients.

The following are the components of The Web Sight Program:

1. **Presenting problems and disorders**
2. **The Web**
   - Ego/Core
   - The Flip
   - Black Box
   - Mirroring
   - De-repression
   - Dismantling the victim identity
   - Tracking the perpetration
   - Incorporating The Web into your program
3. **Interactive drama**
   - Principles of drama therapy
   - The interactive strategy
   - The repertoire of characters
4. **Process Psychology**
   - Group process skills
   - Conflict work
   - World work
   - Racism and privilege

5. **Violence Prevention**
   - The roots of violence
   - The criminal mind
   - The holocaust self
6. **Real Sexuality**
7. **Guild Philosophy**
   - The new ethic
   - Democracy
   - Spirituality
8. **Rites of Passage**
   - Moving from adolescence to adult— the essential lessons
9. **Reading contemporary culture**
10. **Firebelly work**
    - Movement
    - Rhythm
    - Team movement/working in unison on body level

For more information about Hermes' Web or The Web Sight Program, contact:
Jerry Fjerkenstad
Hermes' Web, Ltd.
235 Bedford Street S.E.
Minneapolis, MN 55414
Phone: 612-623-3982
Fax: 612-362-9310
E-mail: jrfnh@aol.com

Jerry Fjerkenstad, M.A., licensed psychologist, is executive director of MASC (Minnesotans Actively Seeking Community) and The Dream Guild Theatre, a nonprofit corporation providing educational and violence and crime prevention services as well as contemporary theater. Jerry is employed as senior clinical supervisor at Project Pathfinder, an outpatient sex offender program in St. Paul, Minnesota. Jerry created Hermes' Web, The Web Sight Program, and the Interactive Drama approach to violence prevention. He is also a writer, actor, pianist, and drummer.

If you would like to have your own model of Hermes' Web,

please fill out the coupon below and mail it to Hermes' Web, Ltd., at the above address. Using this coupon entitles you to purchase a Hermes' Web for $8.00 plus postage & handling—a 33% discount off the retail price. Make your check or money order payable to Hermes' Web. For more information, call 612-623-9310.

detach here --

Please send me a Hermes' Web. Enclosed is my check (or money order) for $8.00, plus $1.50 postage & handling. [Minnesota residents also add 6.5% for state sales tax.] Make check or money order payable to Hermes' Web.

Name: _____

Address: _____

City _____ State: ___ Zip: _____

Phone: _____

E-mail: _____

Notes

CHAPTER 1:

    1. Kimberly S. Young, *Caught in the Net* (New York: John Wiley & Sons, Inc., 1998).

    2. Al Cooper, David L. Delmonico, and Ron Burg, "Cybersex Users, Abusers, and Compulsives: New Findings and Implications," *Sexual Addiction and Compulsivity* 7, nos. 1 and 2 (2000).

CHAPTER 2:

    1. Jennifer P. Schneider, "Sexual Addiction: Controversy in Mainstream Medicine, Diagnosis Based on the DSM-III-R and Physician Case Histories," *Sexual Addiction and Compulsivity* 1, no. 1 (1994): 19–44.

    2. David Delmonico, published on the Internet at www.sexhelp.com (1999).

CHAPTER 3:

    1. James O. Prochaska, John C. Norcross, and Carlos C. DiClemente, *Changing for Good* (New York: Avon Books, 1995).

    2. G. Alan Marlatt and Judith R. Gordon, eds., *Relapse Prevention: Maintenance Strategies in the Treatment of Addictive Behaviors* (New York: Guilford Press, 1985).

CHAPTER 5:

    1. Patrick J. Carnes, *Facing the Shadow* (Wickenburg, Ariz.: Gentle Path Press, 2001).

    2. Patrick J. Carnes, *Contrary to Love* (Center City, Minn.: Hazelden, 1989).

    3. Patrick J. Carnes, *Facing the Shadow* (Wickenburg, Ariz.: Gentle Path Press, 2001).

    4. G. Alan Marlatt and Judith R. Gordon, eds., *Relapse Prevention: Maintenance Strategies in the Treatment of Addictive Behaviors* (New York: Guilford Press, 1985).

CHAPTER 6

    1. The use of Hermes' Web as a tool for addiction recovery was developed by Jerry Fjerkenstad. All information on Hermes' Web used with permission. (See appendix for more information.)

    2. Patrick J. Carnes, *Sexual Anorexia: Overcoming Sexual Self-Hatred* (Center City, Minn: Hazelden, 1997).

    3. Daniel Goleman, *Emotional Intelligence: Why It Can Matter More Than IQ* (New York: Bantam Book, 1995).

    4. Patrick Carnes, *Don't Call It Love: Recovery from Sexual Addiction* (Phoenix, Ariz.: Gentle Path Press, 1991).

About the Authors

David Delmonico, Ph.D., is an assistant professor in the Department of Counseling, Psychology, and Special Education at Duquesne University in Pittsburgh, Pennsylvania. He is a graduate of Kent State University with degrees in community counseling, psychology, and counseling and human development services. He has worked and published numerous articles in the area of sexual addiction over the past ten years.

Elizabeth Griffin, M.A., is a licensed marriage and family therapist with more than fifteen years of experience treating sexual disorders. She has worked in outpatient, inpatient, military, and prison settings. She lectures nationally on the assessment and treatment of sexual disorders as well as cybersex issues relating to those with sexual disorders. She is currently chief operating officer for the American Foundation for Addiction Research, a nonprofit organization dedicated to fostering scientific research and understanding and disseminating knowledge of the nature and causes of addictive disorders.

Joseph Moriarity, B.A., B.S., has worked for over twenty years as a freelance writer with a primary focus in the fields of health care, addiction and treatment, science, and education. He has previously ghostwritten three other books for Hazelden, *Winning a Day at a Time* with John Lucas, *Sexual Anorexia* with Patrick Carnes, and *In the Shadows of the Net: Breaking Free of Compulsive Online Sexual Behavior* with Patrick Carnes, David Delmonico, and Elizabeth Griffin.